CROSS STITCH
HAPPY ANIMALS
32 DRAWING OF ANIMALS CROSS STITCH

PUNTO DE CRUZ
ANIMALES FELICES
32 DIBUJOS DE ANIMALES DE PUNTO DE CRUZ

Welcome!

Welcome to this wonderful world of cross-stitch, where every stitch tells a story and every pattern comes to life with the touch of your needle. In this book, we embark on a fascinating journey through the animal kingdom, exploring a diversity of creatures that you can recreate with threads and fabric.

From the majestic lions of the savannah to the tiny hummingbirds buzzing among the flowers, each design has been carefully crafted to capture the essence and charm of these marvelous beings. Whether you are a beginner in the art of cross-stitch or an experienced enthusiast, you will find patterns that inspire and challenge you.

Cross-stitch is not just a technique; it is a form of artistic expression that has endured through the centuries. With each project, you will have the opportunity to perfect your skills, learn new techniques, and, above all, enjoy the creative process. This book is designed to provide you with a clear and detailed guide, with step-by-step instructions and helpful tips to ensure your projects are a success.

So, prepare your colored threads, your needle, and your fabric, and get ready to embark on a creative adventure. Let these animal patterns transport you to a world full of beauty and detail, where every stitch brings you a little closer to nature.

Happy stitching!

¡Bienvenido!

Bienvenidos a este maravilloso mundo del punto de cruz, donde cada puntada cuenta una historia y cada patrón cobra vida con el toque de tu aguja. En este libro, nos embarcamos en un viaje fascinante a través del reino animal, explorando una diversidad de criaturas que podrás recrear con hilos y tela.

Desde los majestuosos leones de la sabana hasta los pingüinos que corretean por el hielo, cada diseño ha sido cuidadosamente elaborado para capturar la esencia y el encanto de estos seres maravillosos. Tanto si eres un principiante en el arte del punto de cruz como si eres un aficionado experimentado, encontrarás patrones que te inspirarán y desafiarán.

El punto de cruz no es solo una técnica, es una forma de expresión artística que ha perdurado a lo largo de los siglos. Con cada proyecto, tendrás la oportunidad de perfeccionar tus habilidades, aprender nuevas técnicas y, sobre todo, disfrutar del proceso creativo. Este libro está diseñado para proporcionarte una guía clara y detallada, con instrucciones paso a paso y consejos útiles para asegurar que tus proyectos sean un éxito.

Así que prepara tus hilos de colores, tu aguja y tu tela, y prepárate para embarcarte en una aventura creativa. Deja que estos patrones de animales te transporten a un mundo lleno de belleza y detalle, donde cada puntada te acerca un poco más a la naturaleza.

¡Feliz bordado!

Glossary / Glosario

English	Español
Design size	Tamaño del diseño
Puntadas	Puntadas
Floss list for crosses	Lista de hilos
Use 2 Strands of thread for cross stitch	Usa 2 hilos de hilo para punto de cruz
Symbol	Simbolo
Number	Número
Name	Nombre

Material to use / Material a utilizar

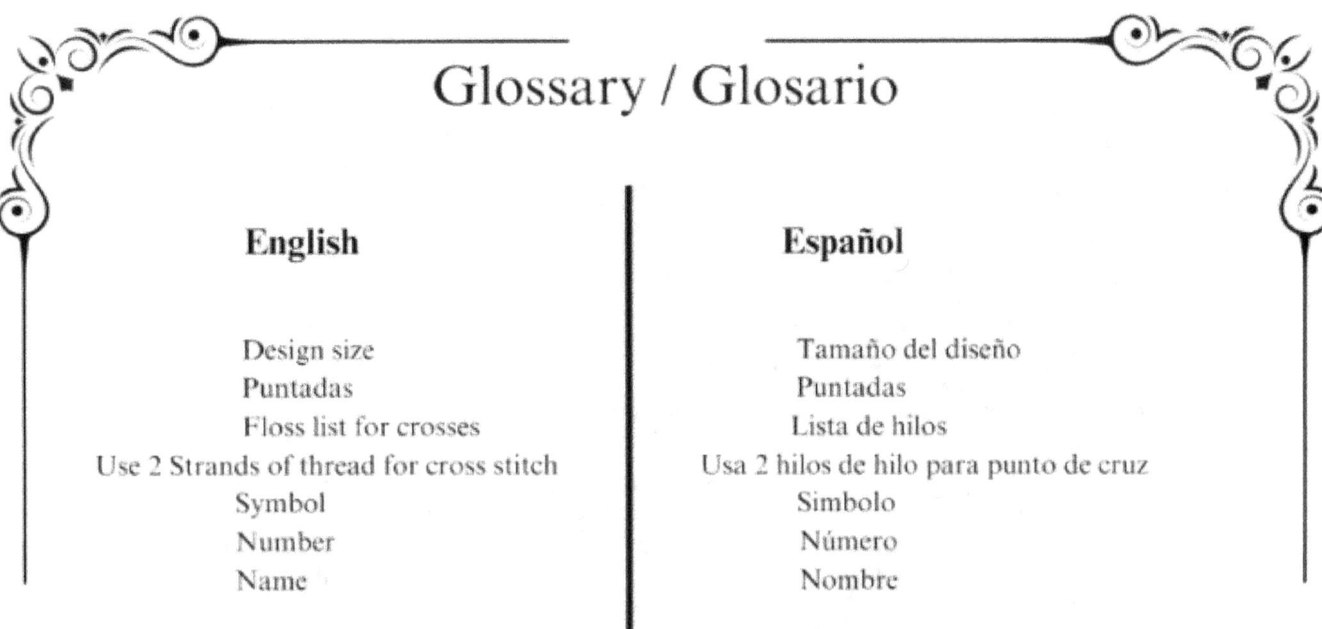

Thread DMC / Hilo DMC

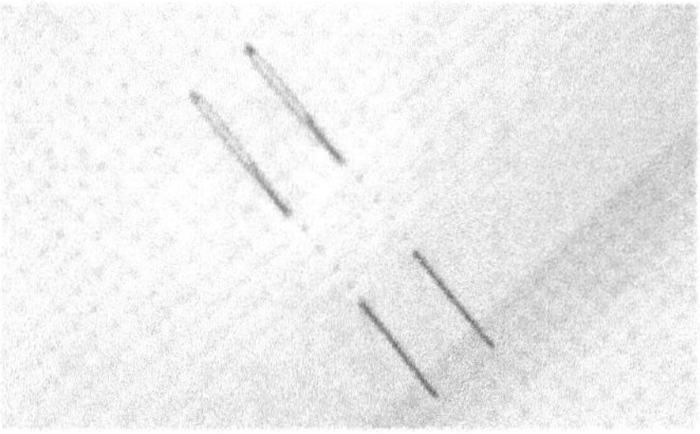

Needles / agujas

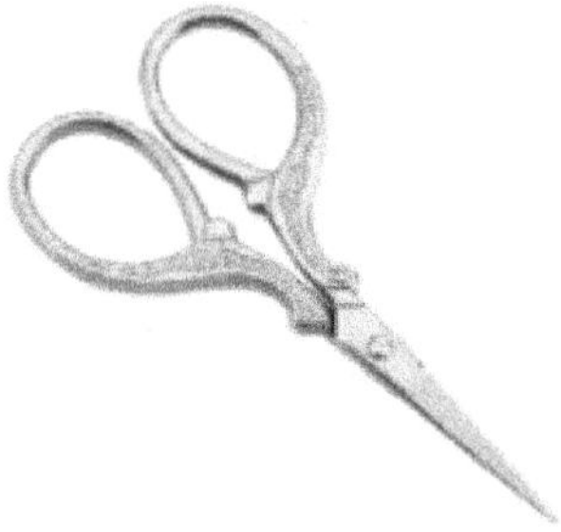

Scissors / Tijeras

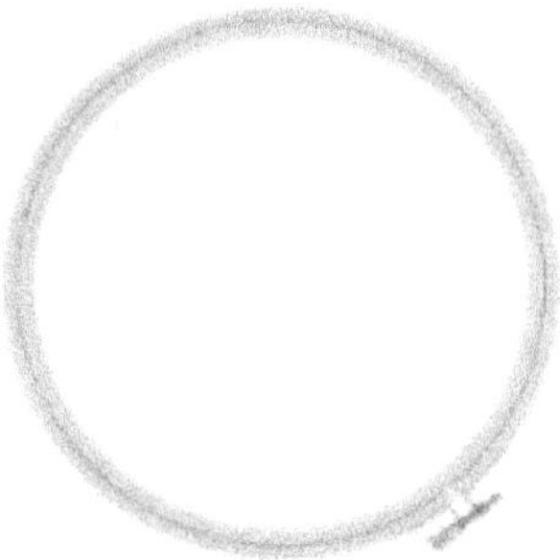

Hoop / Aro

Fabric / Tela

Owl / Búho

Design size: 85 x 85 stitches

Floss list for crosses

Use 2 strands of thread for cross stitch

N	Symbol		Number	Name	Stitches
1	☆	☆	DMC 20	Shrimp	150
2	∠	∠	DMC 211	Lavender - Light	1387
3	m	m	DMC 356	Terra Cotta - Medium	454
4	=	=	DMC 402	Mahogany - Very Light	475
5	⌐	⌐	DMC 444	Lemon - Dark	96
6	♡	♡	DMC 746	Off White	336
7	♣	♣	DMC 918	Red Copper - Dark	982
8	✕	✕	DMC 922	Copper - Light	40
9	◯	◯	DMC 950	Desert Sand - Light	666
10	✳	✳	DMC 957	Geranium - Pale	46

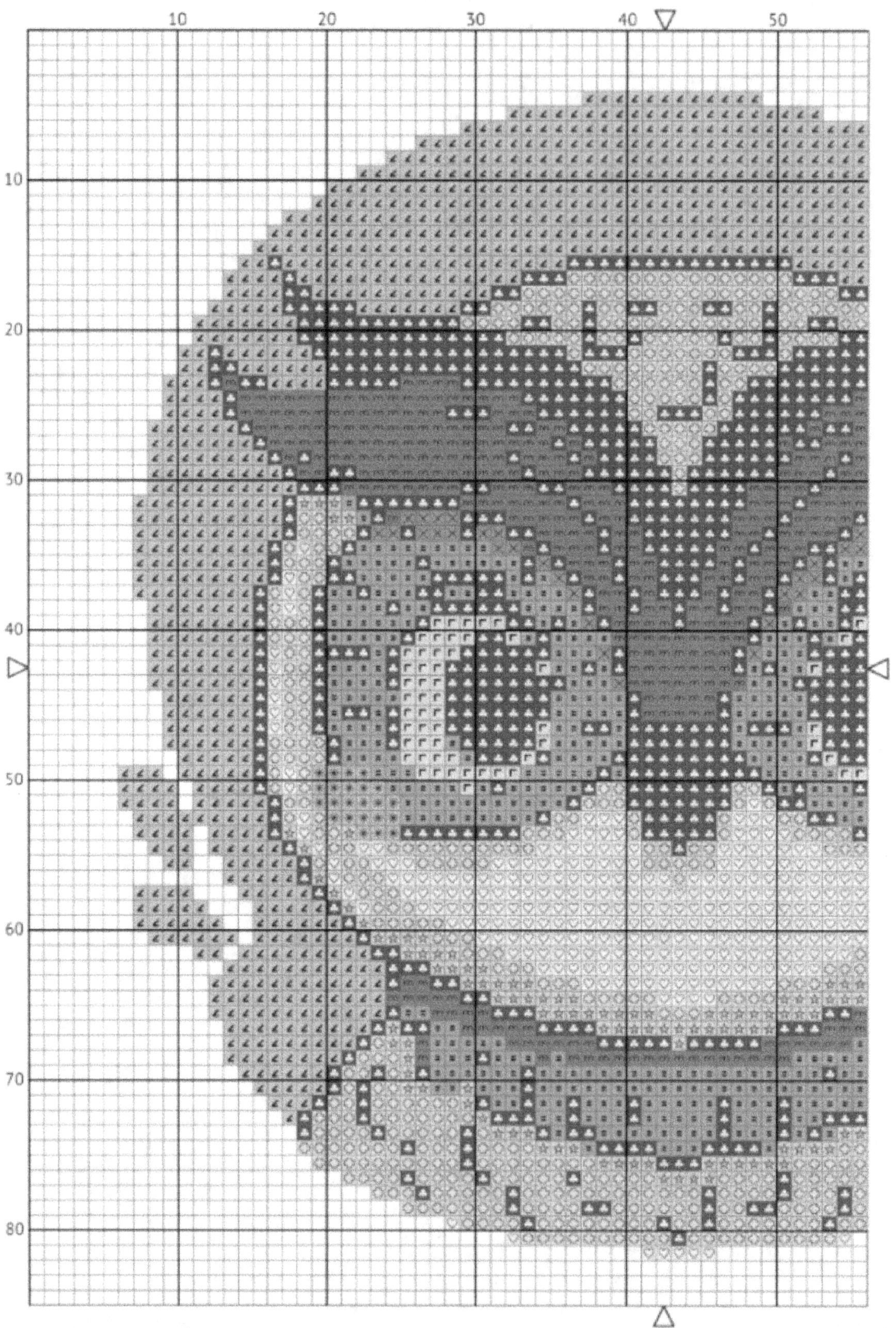

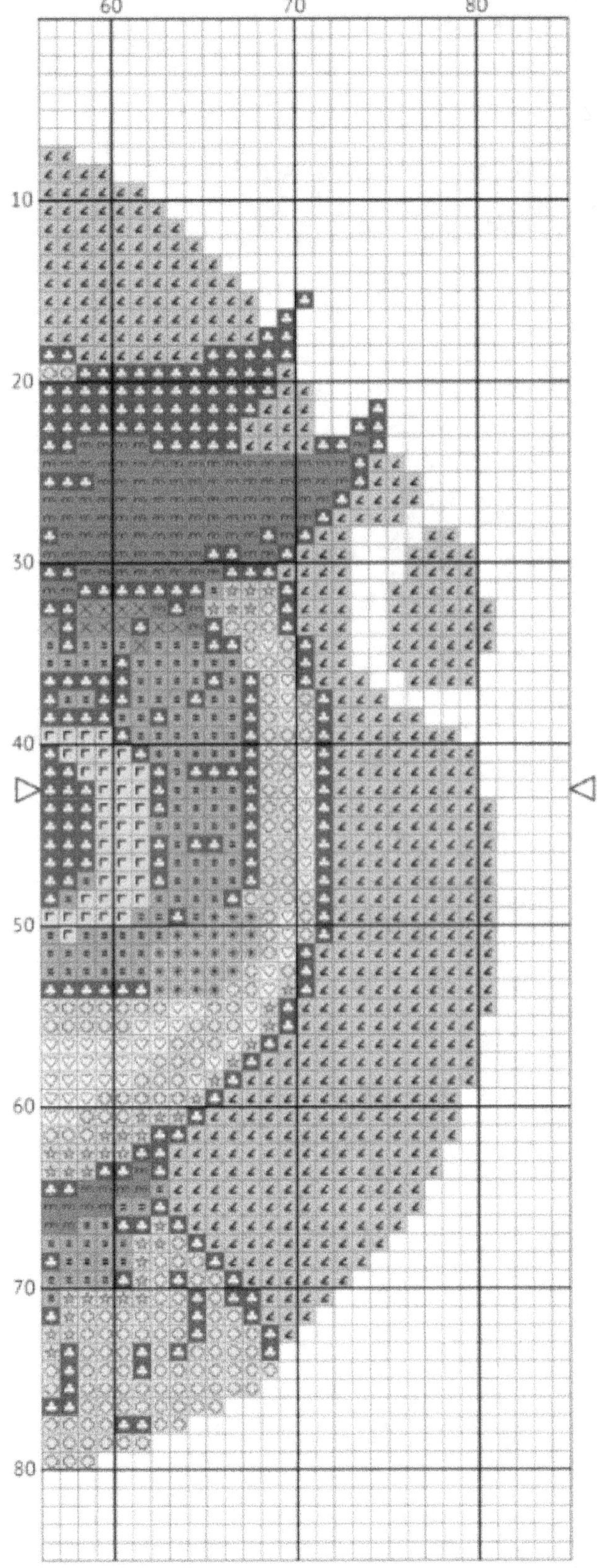

Pig / Cerdo

Design size: 85 x 81 stitches

Floss list for crosses

Use 2 strands of thread for cross stitch

N	Symbol		Number	Name	Stitches
1	✕	✕	DMC B5200	Snow White	100
2	♡	♡	DMC 20	Shrimp	395
3	◺	◺	DMC 210	Lavender - Medium	1568
4	∠	∠	DMC 225	Shell Pink - Ultra Very Light	184
5	m	m	DMC 918	Red Copper - Dark	375
6	♣	♣	DMC 950	Desert Sand - Light	1803
7	◊	◊	DMC 957	Geranium - Pale	58

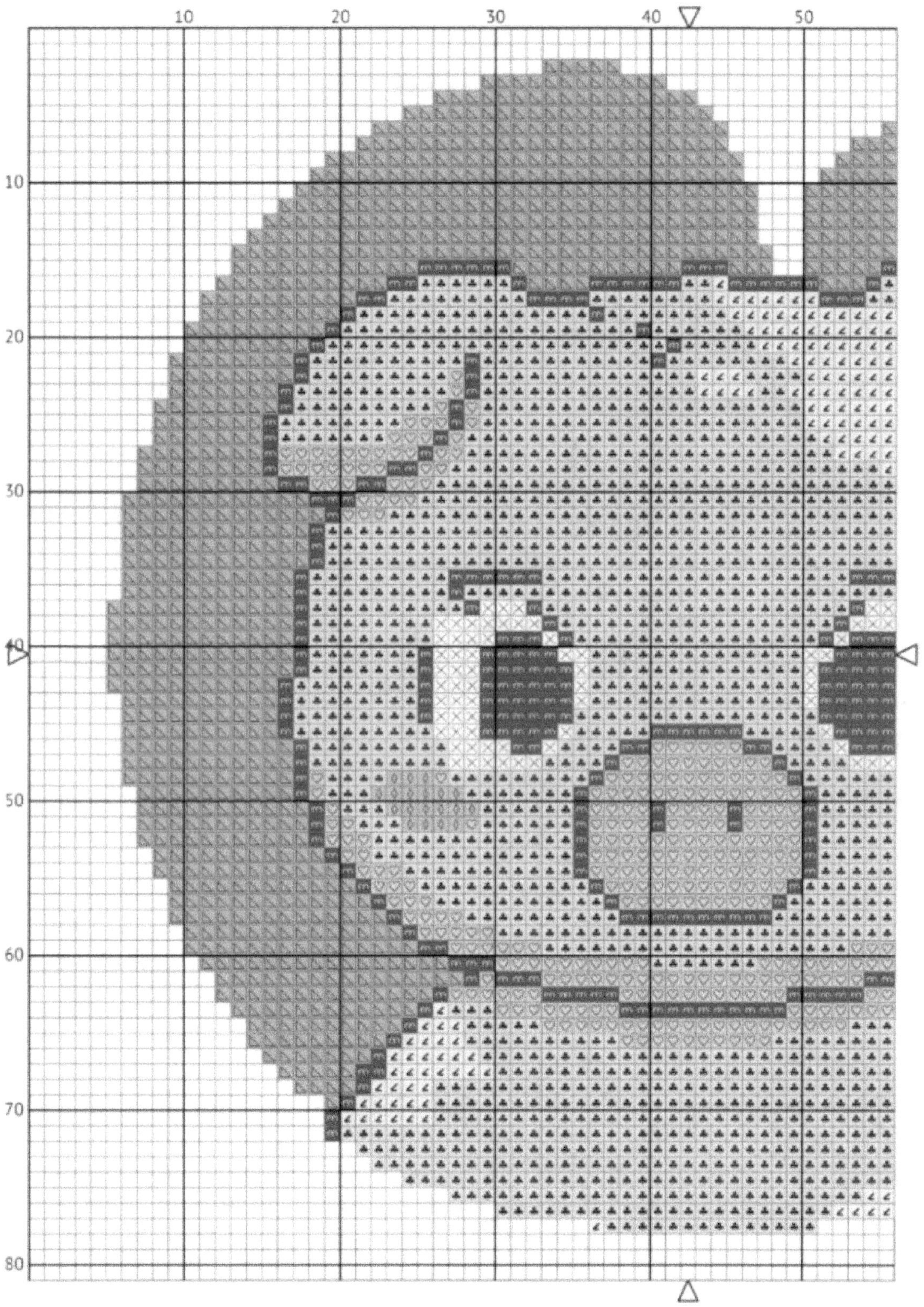

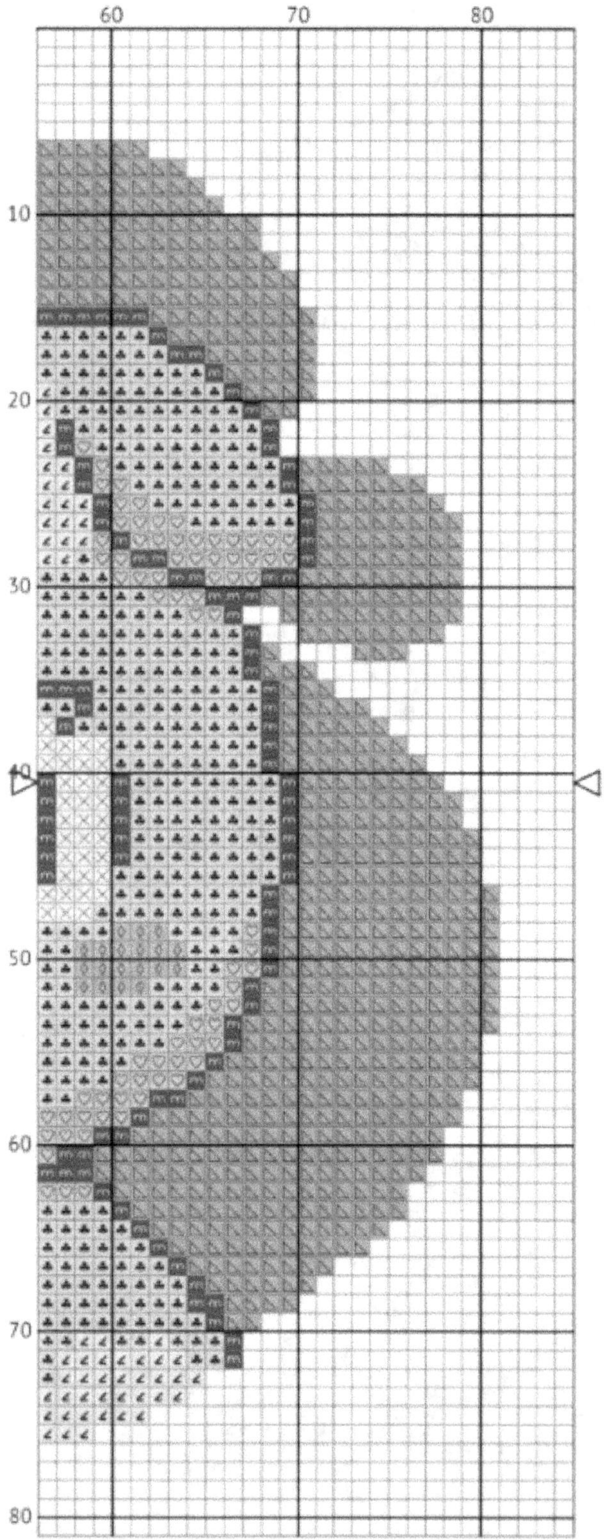

Crocodile / Cocodrilo

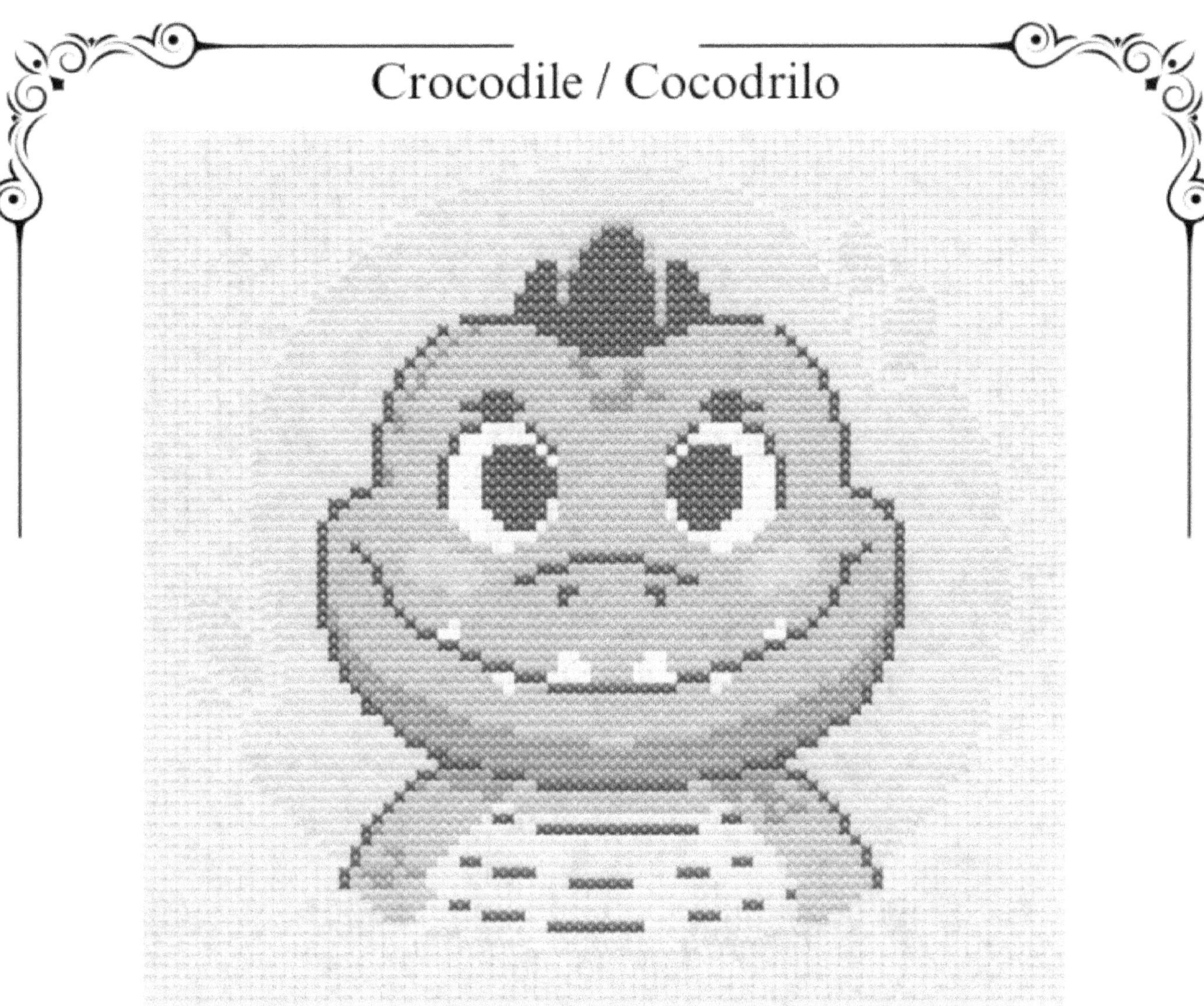

Design size: 85 x 81 stitches

Floss list for crosses

Use 2 strands of thread for cross stitch

N	Symbol		Number	Name	Stitches
1	◊	◊	DMC B5200	Snow White	130
2	■	■	DMC 14	Apple Green - Pale	334
3	●	●	DMC 745	Yellow - Light Pale	1467
4	♡	♥	DMC 909	Emerald Green - Very Dark	556
5	♣	♣	DMC 912	Emerald Green - Light	266
6	∠	∠	DMC 954	Nile Green	1379
7	≡	≡	DMC 967	Apricot - Very Light	48

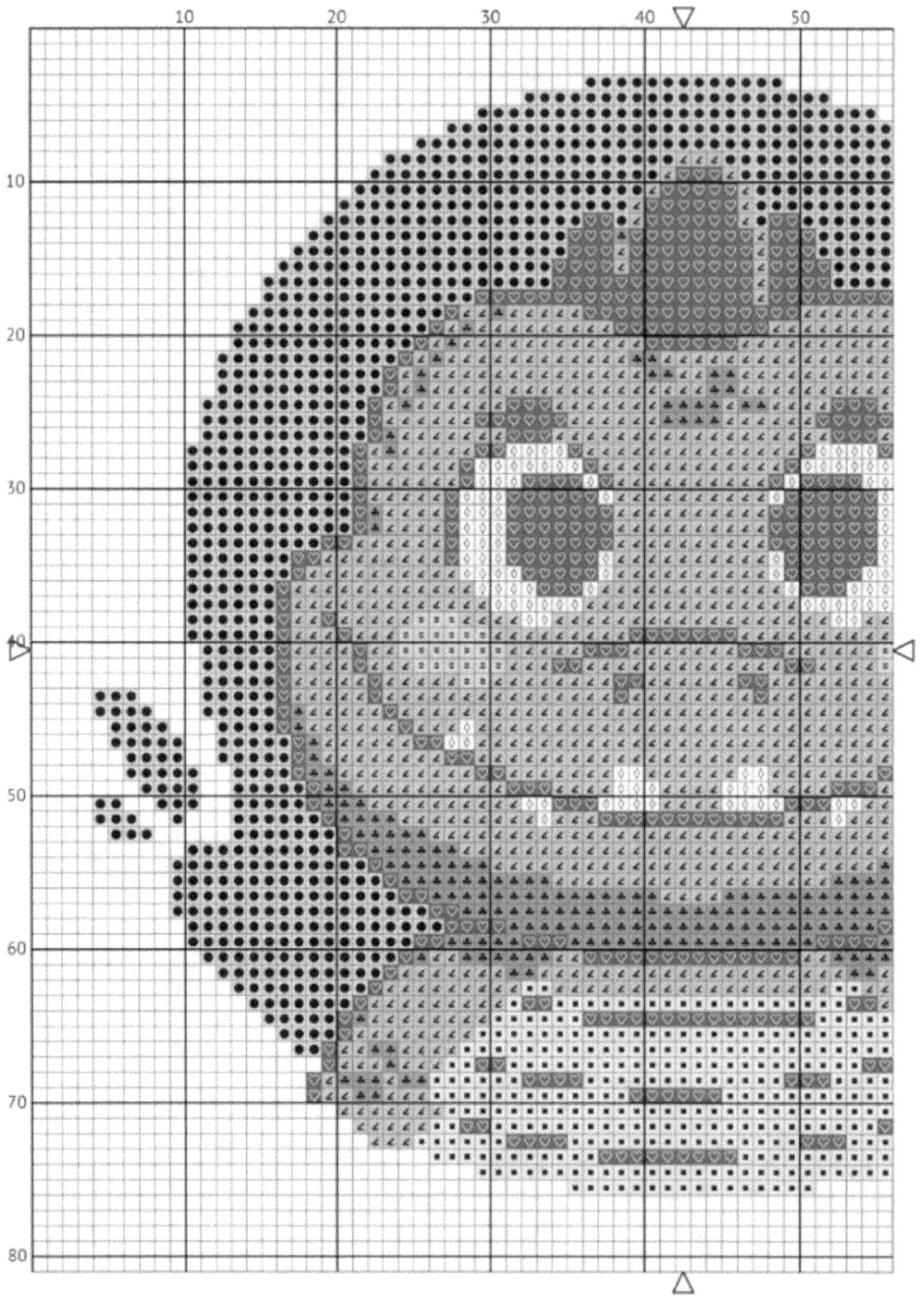

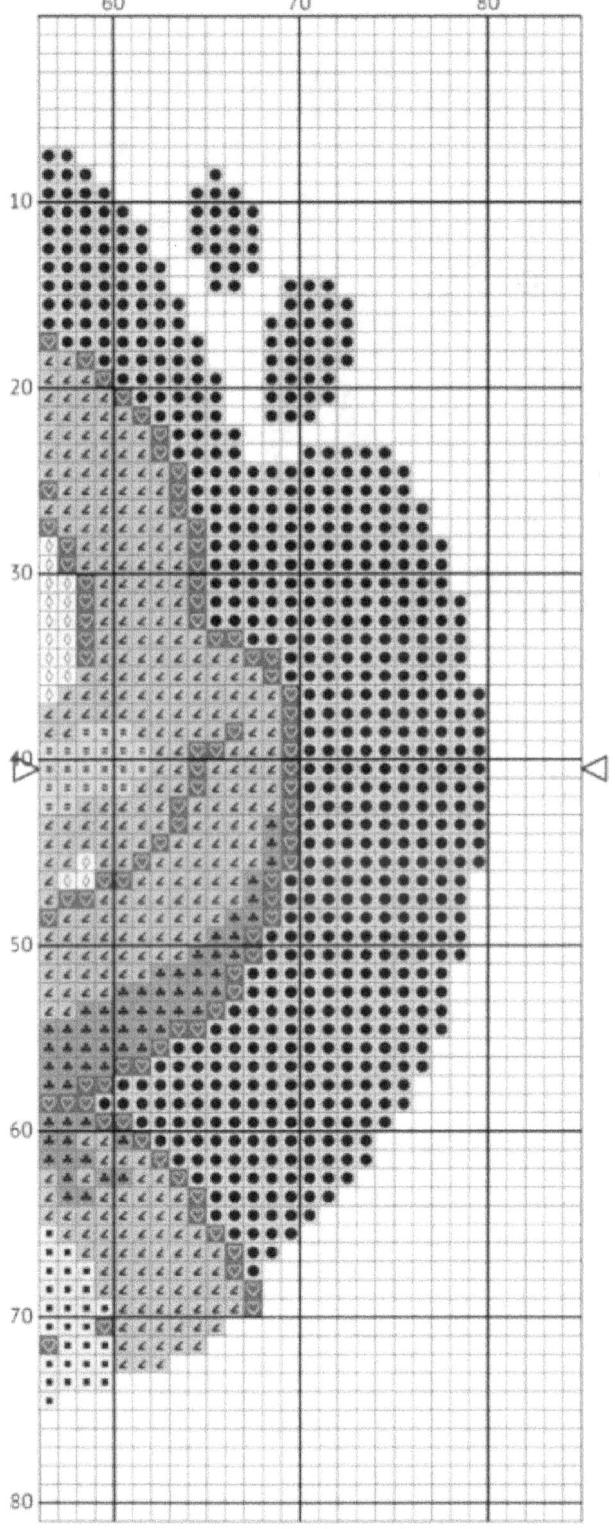

Rabbit / Conejo

Design size: 85 x 89 stitches

Floss list for crosses

Use 2 strands of thread for cross stitch

N	Symbol		Number	Name	Stitches
1	✕	✕	DMC B5200	Snow White	479
2	♣	♣	DMC BLANK	White	2755
3	●	●	DMC 25	Lavender - Ultra Light	312
4	◺	◺	DMC 162	Blue - Ultra Very Light	1069
5	✿	✿	DMC 3689	Mauve - Light	127
6	◢	◢	DMC 3807	Cornflower Blue	542

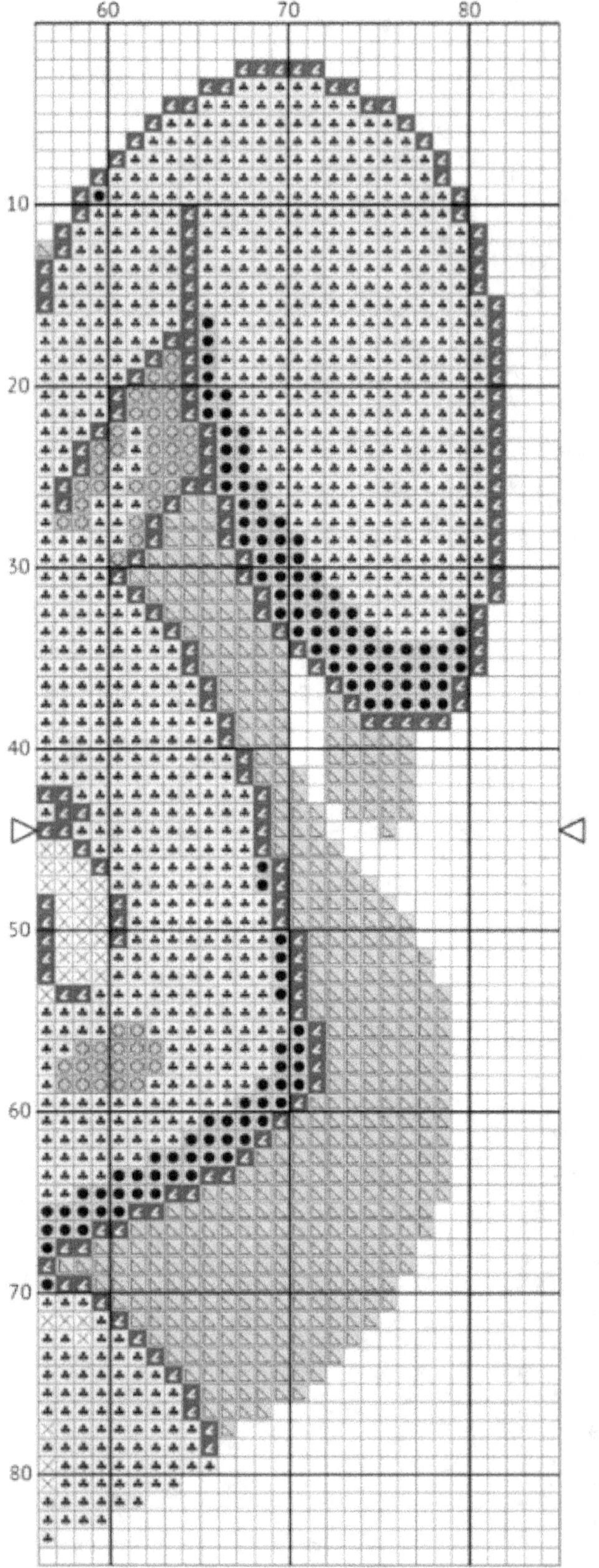

Elephant / Elefante

Design size: 85 x 73 stitches

Floss list for crosses

Use 2 strands of thread for cross stitch

N	Symbol		Number	Name	Stitches
1	✕	✕	DMC B5200	Snow White	60
2	▽	▽	DMC 24	Lavender - White	1208
3	■	■	DMC 211	Lavender - Light	438
4	○	○	DMC 552	Violet - Medium	425
5	●	●	DMC 963	Dusty Rose - Ultra Very Light	754
6	◣	◣	DMC 3326	Rose - Light	622
7	◺	◺	DMC 3689	Mauve - Light	156

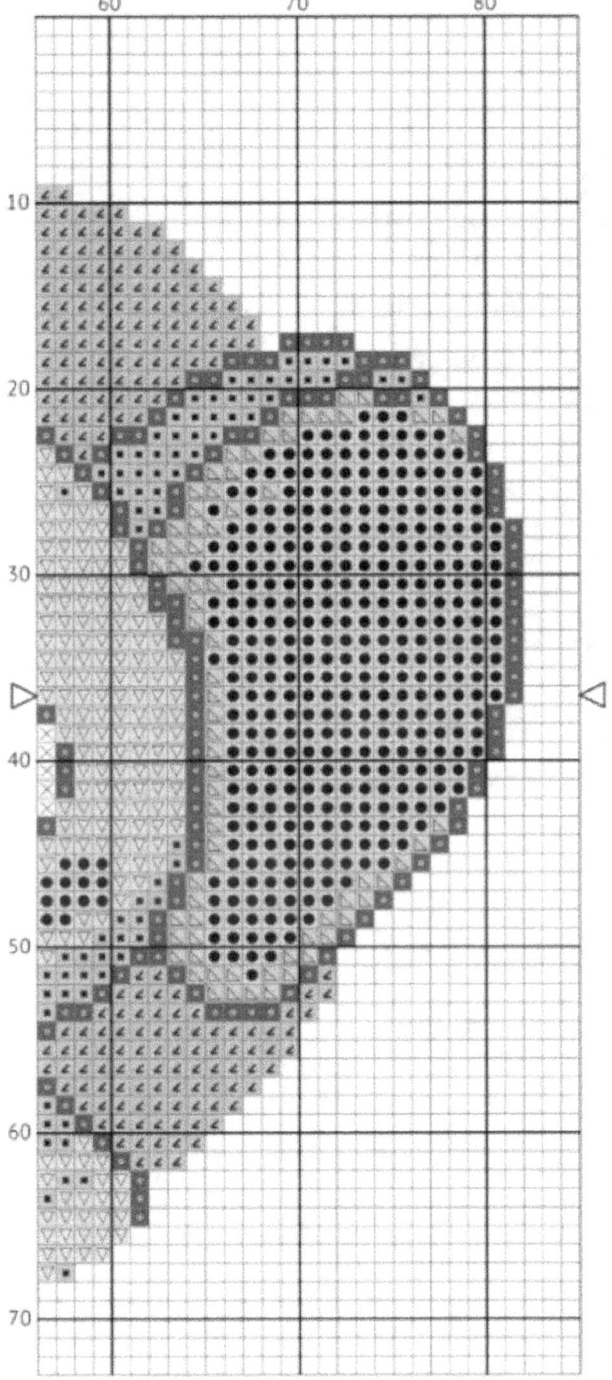

Porcupine / Puerco Espín

Design size: 85 x 84 stitches

Floss list for crosses

Use 2 strands of thread for cross stitch

N	Symbol		Number	Name	Stitches
1	⌐	⌐	DMC B5200	Snow White	86
2	■	■	DMC 746	Off White	264
3	○	○	DMC 814	Garnet - Dark	558
4	▽	▽	DMC 919	Red Copper	635
5	m	m	DMC 957	Geranium - Pale	34
6	●	●	DMC 967	Apricot - Very Light	181
7	♡	♡	DMC 3774	Desert Sand - Very Light	1329
8	∠	∠	DMC 3779	Rosewood - Very Light	810
9	◺	◺	DMC 3830	Terra Cotta	772

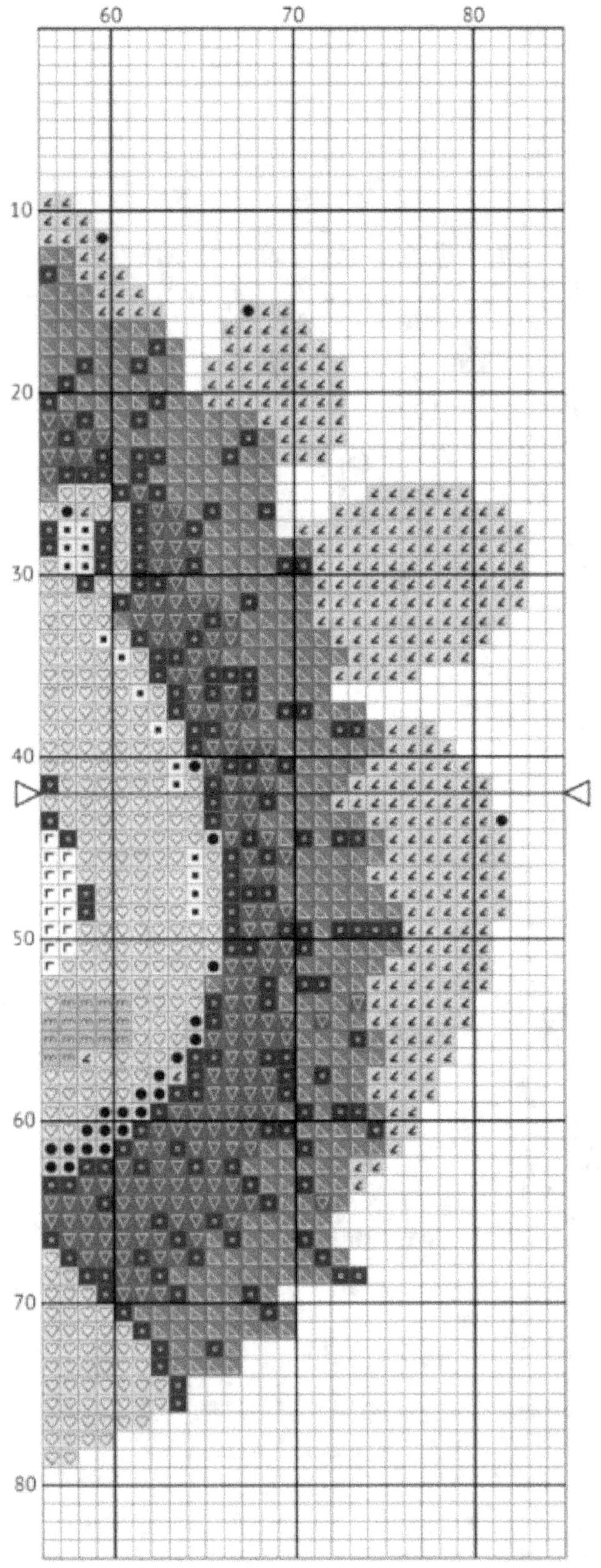

Skunk / Mofeta

Design size: 85 x 80 stitches

Floss list for crosses

Use 2 strands of thread for cross stitch

N	Symbol		Number	Name	Stitches
1	○	○	DMC B5200	Snow White	92
2	≡	≡	DMC 30	Blueberry - Medium Light	174
3	○	○	DMC 32	Blueberry - Dark	278
4	▽	▽	DMC 168	Pewter - Very Light	119
5	✕	✕	DMC 3747	Blue Violet - Very Light	50
6	✳	✳	DMC 3779	Rosewood - Very Light	40
7	☆	☆	DMC 3807	Cornflower Blue	789
8	♣	♣	DMC BLANK	White	1086
9	◁	◁	DMC 336	Navy Blue	491
10	◢	◢	DMC 955	Nile Green - Light	1291

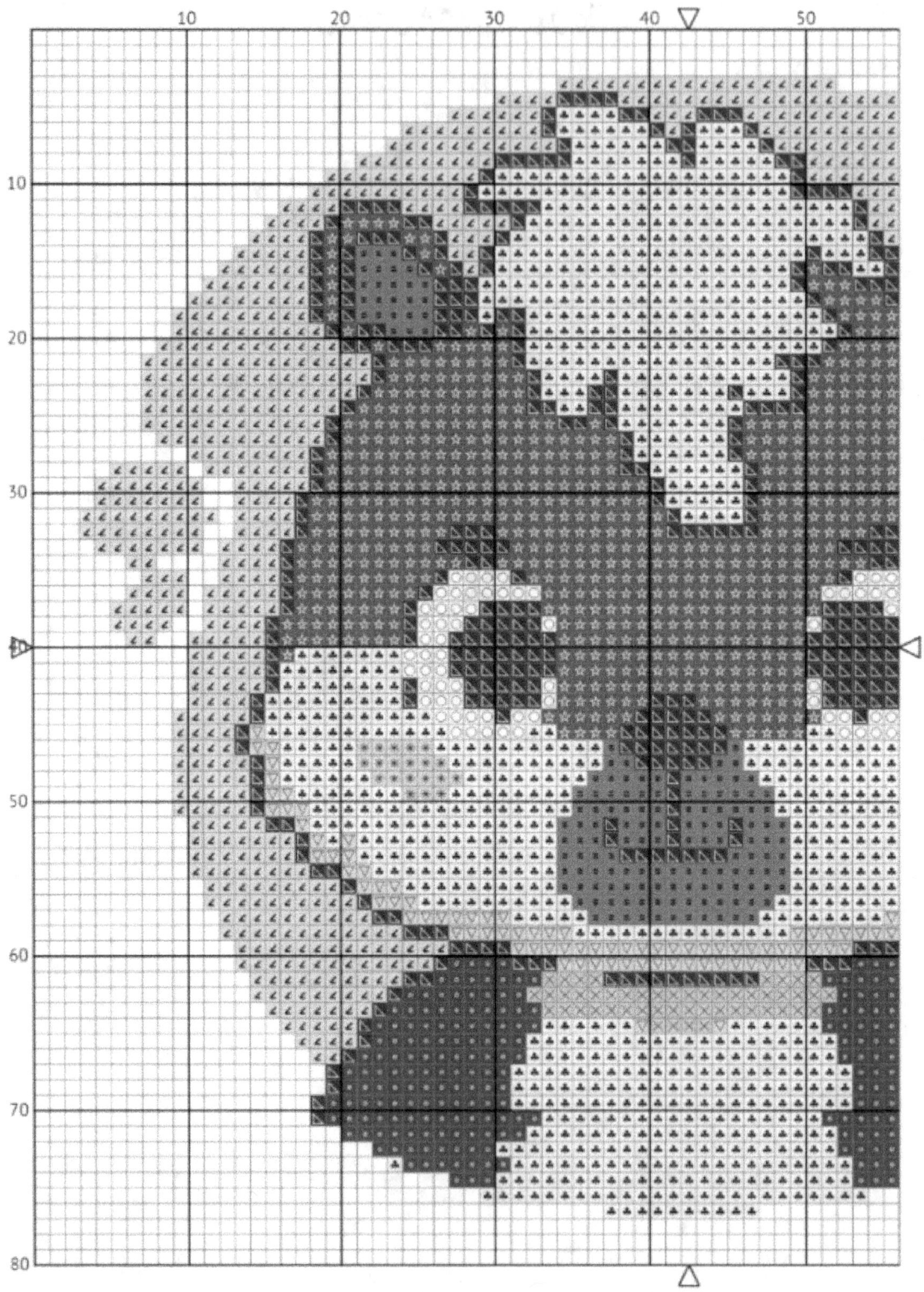

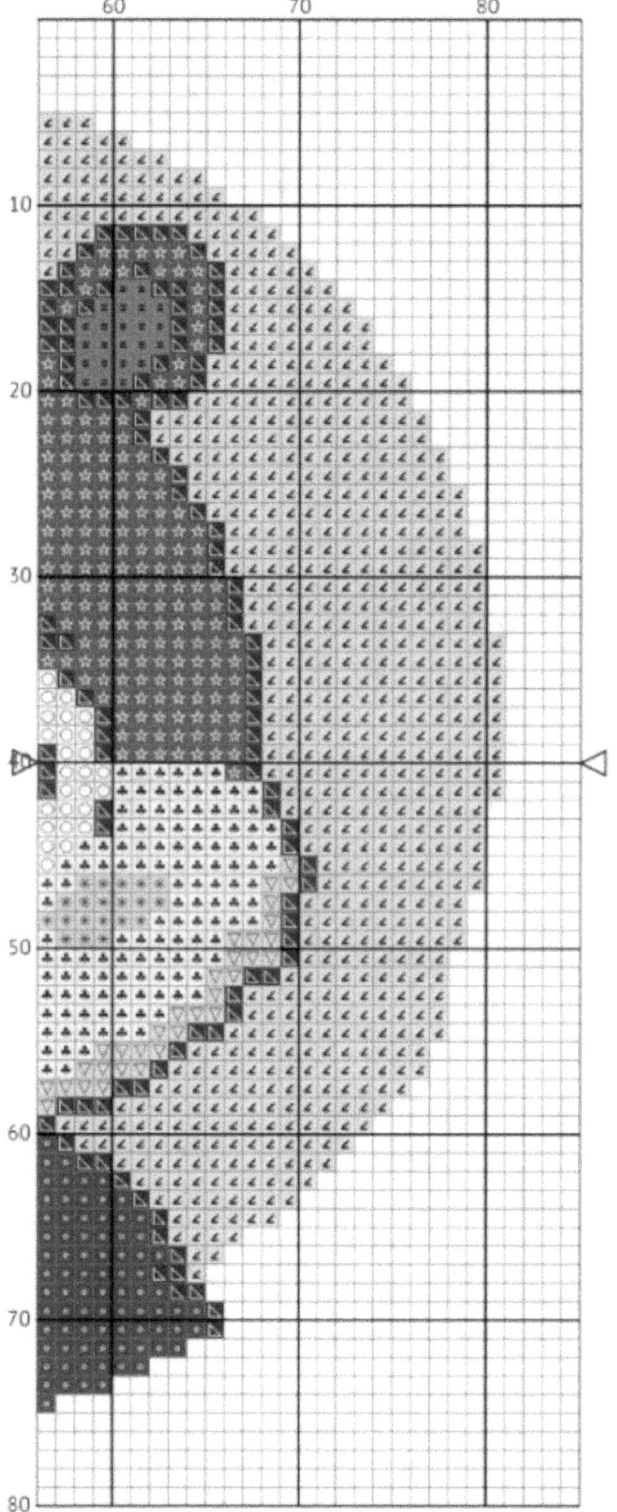

Fowl / Gallina

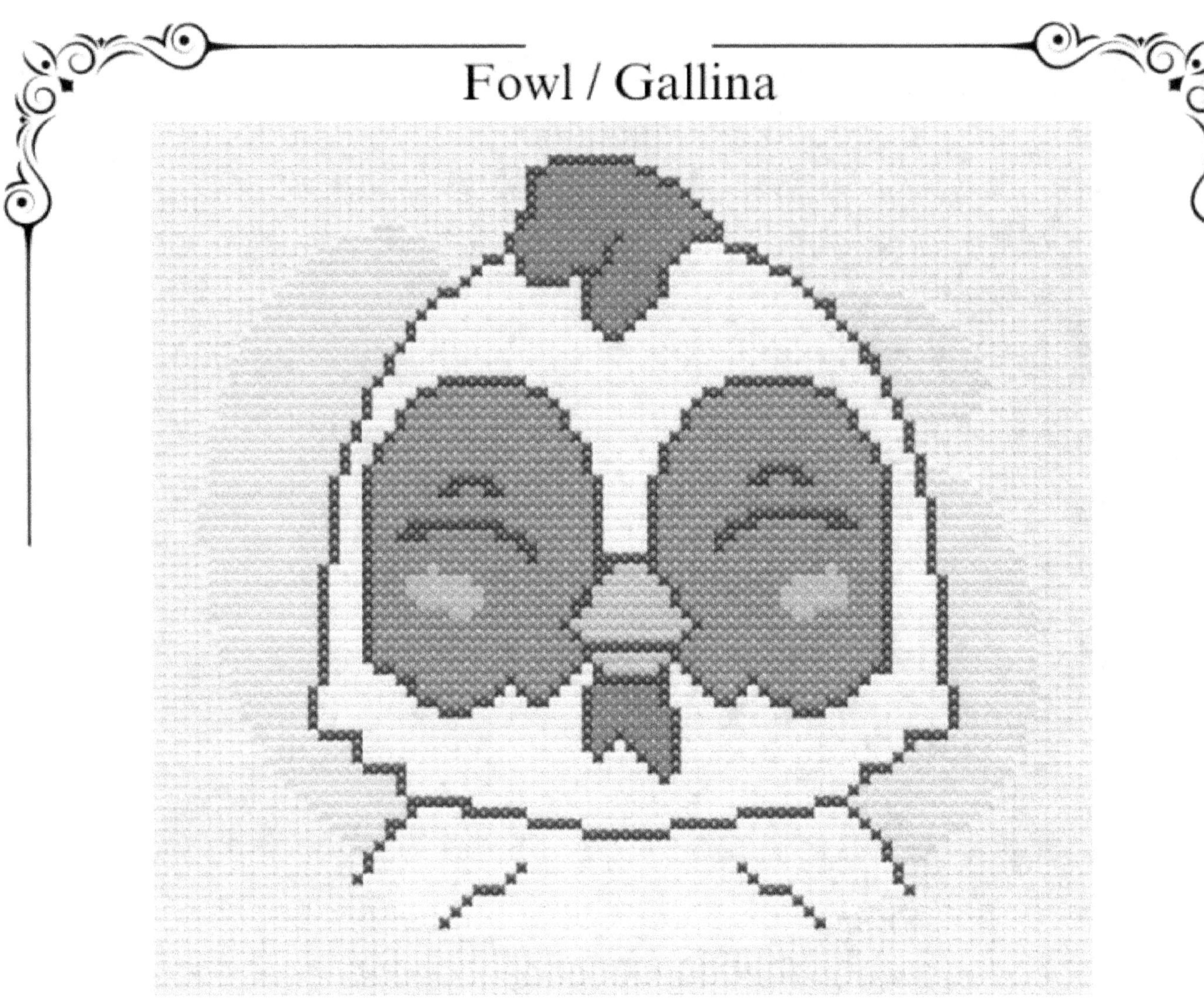

Design size: 85 x 79 stitches

Floss list for crosses

Use 2 strands of thread for cross stitch

N	Symbol		Number	Name	Stitches
1	▽	▽	DMC 21	Alizarín - Light	874
2	♡	♡	DMC 349	Coral - Dark	190
3	■	■	DMC 745	Yellow - Light Pale	962
4	m	m	DMC 746	Off White	1538
5	●	◯	DMC 918	Red Copper - Dark	501
6	◇	◇	DMC 957	Geranium - Pale	42
7	☆	☆	DMC 3827	Golden Brown - Pale	63

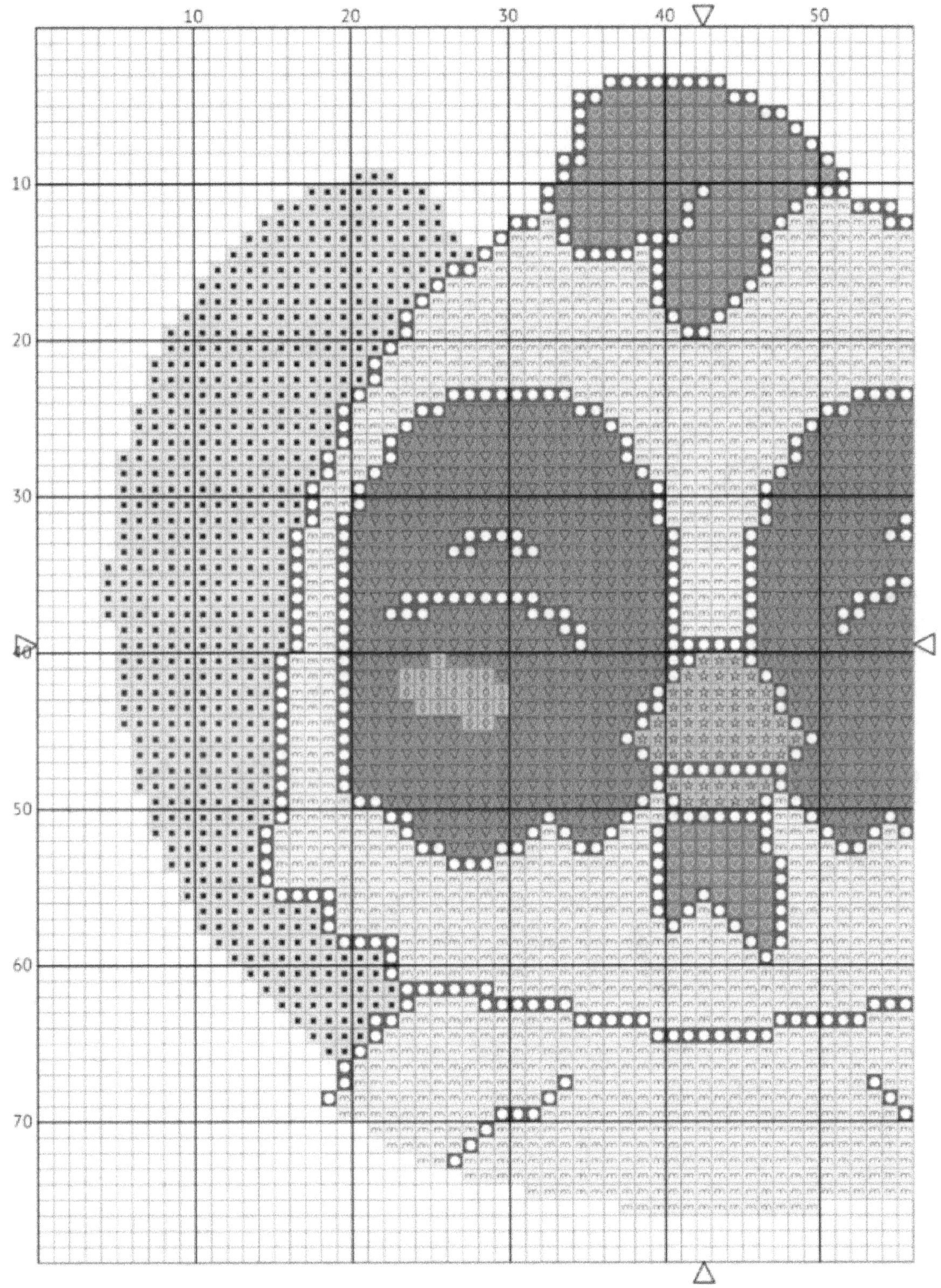

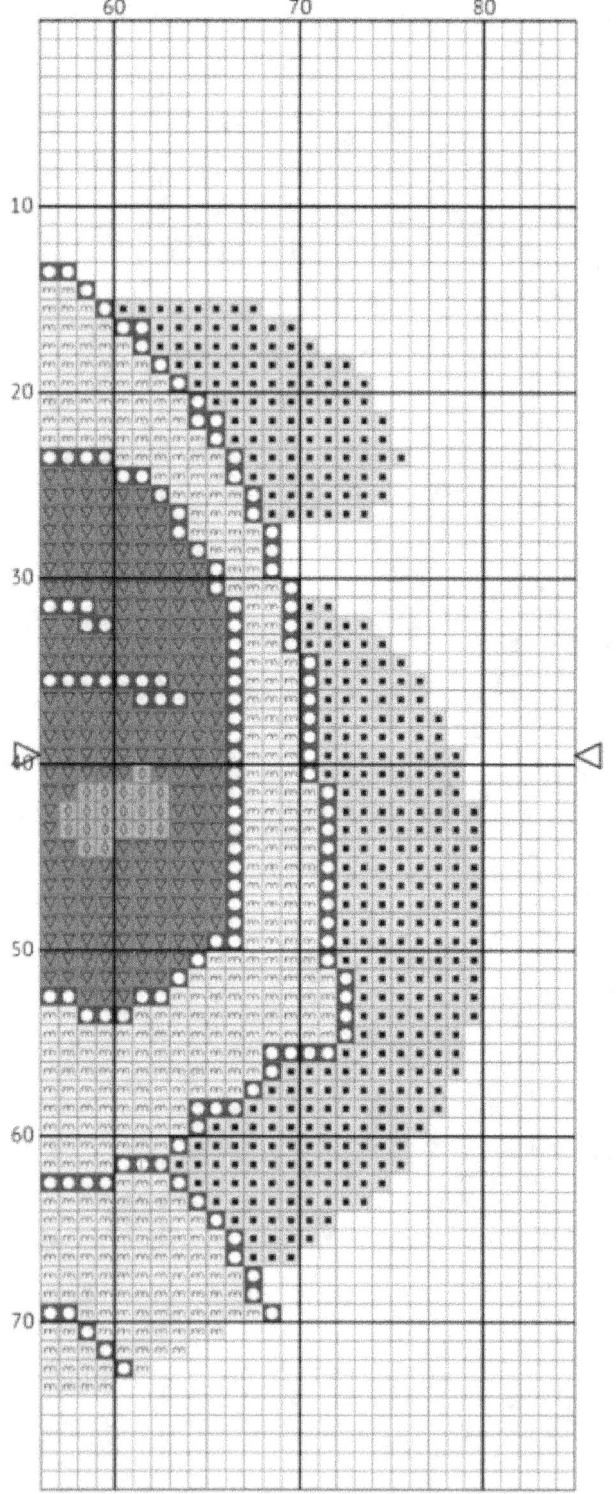

Hippo / Hipopótamo

Design size: 85 x 82 stitches

Floss list for crosses

Use 2 strands of thread for cross stitch

N	Symbol		Number	Name	Stitches
1	♯	♯	DMC B5200	Snow White	107
2	☆	☆	DMC 24	Lavender - White	1847
3	≡	≡	DMC 211	Lavender - Light	282
4	m	m	DMC 327	Violet - Dark	467
5	✕	✕	DMC 963	Dusty Rose - Ultra Very Light	80
6	●	●	DMC 3753	Antique Blue - Ultra Very Light	1649

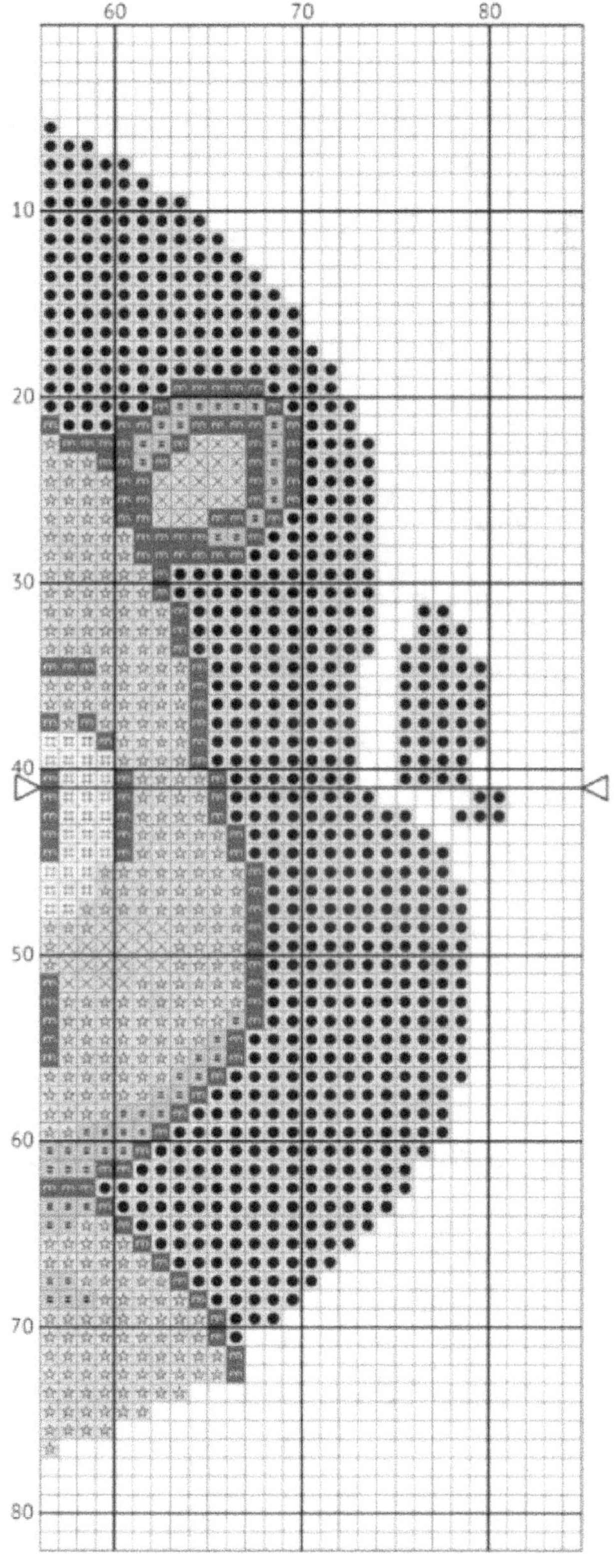

Wild Pig / Jabalí

Floss list for crosses

Use 2 strands of thread for cross stitch

N	Symbol		Number	Name	Stitches
1	◊	◊	DMC B5200	Snow White	108
2	●	●	DMC 24	Lavender - White	1305
3	✿	✿	DMC 30	Blueberry - Medium Light	66
4	○	○	DMC 336	Navy Blue	237
5	∠	∠	DMC 746	Off White	26
6	◺	◺	DMC 823	Navy Blue - Dark	843
7	▽	▽	DMC 3689	Mauve - Light	188
8	m	m	DMC 3807	Cornflower Blue	1949

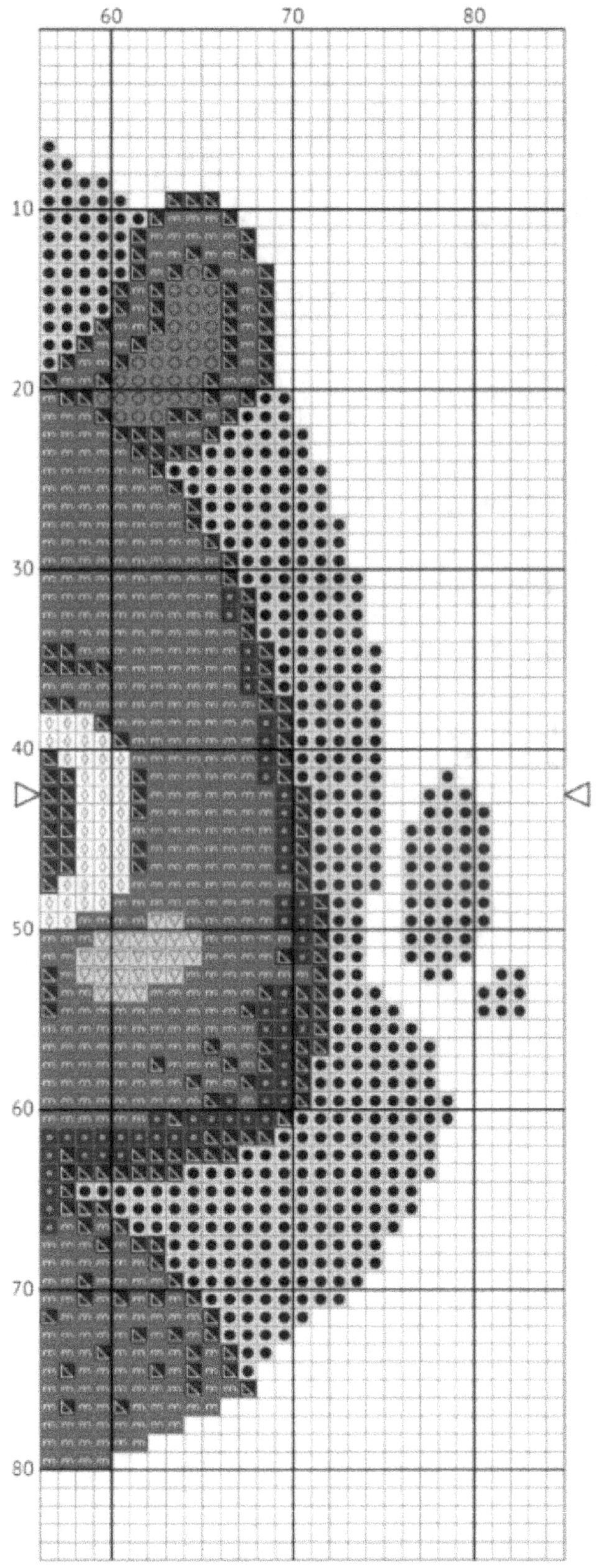

Giraffe / Jirafa

Design size: 85 x 78 stitches

Floss list for crosses

Use 2 strands of thread for cross stitch

N	Symbol		Number	Name	Stitches
1	≡	≡	DMC 19	Autumn Gold - Medium Light	723
2	◺	◺	DMC 22	Alizarin	548
3	♡	♡	DMC 355	Terra Cotta - Dark	113
4	◊	◊	DMC 746	Off White	1212
5	m	m	DMC 747	Sky Blue - Very Light	937
6	●	○	DMC 902	Garnet - Very Dark	456
7	♣	♣	DMC 3779	Rosewood - Very Light	38

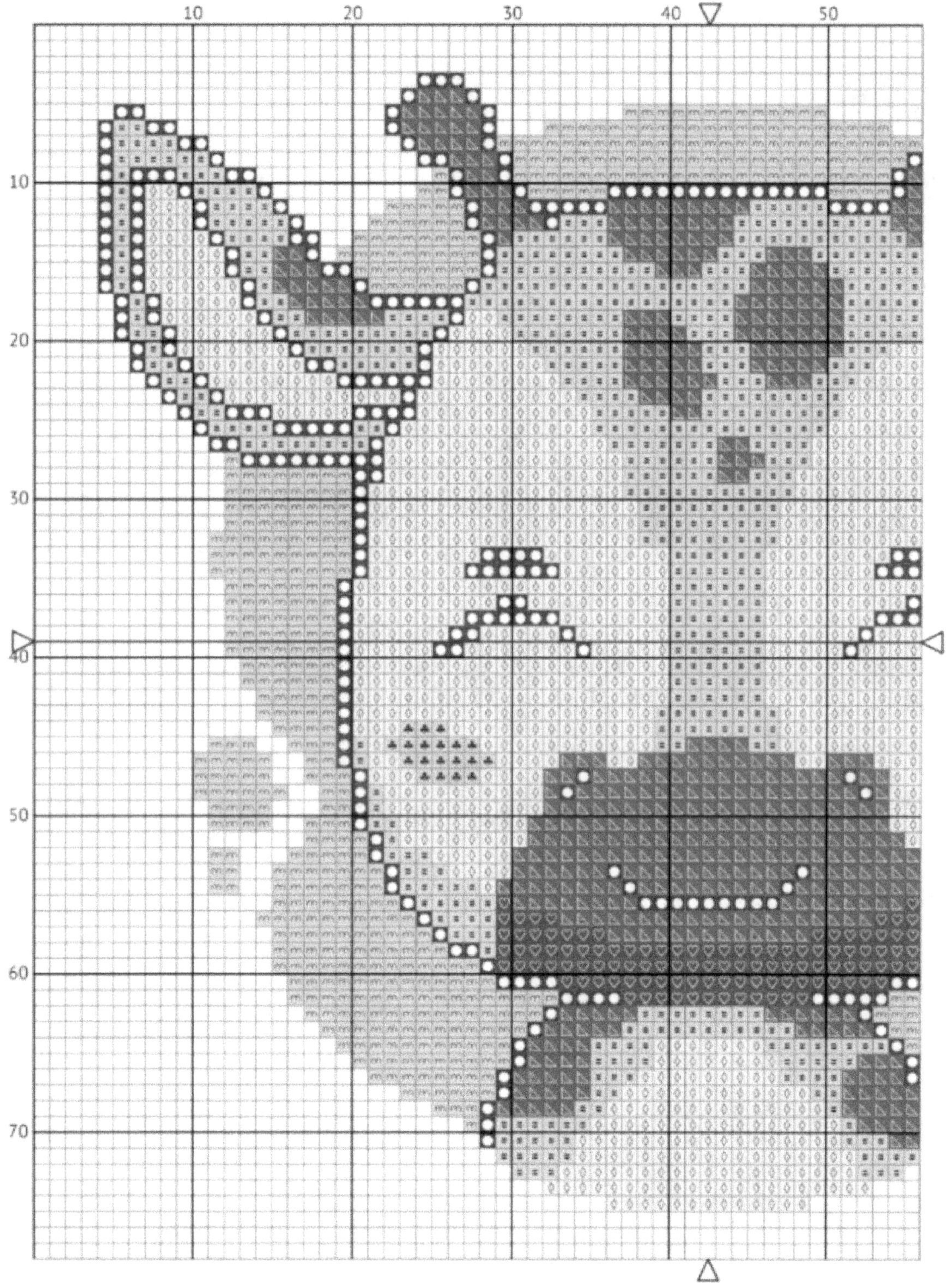

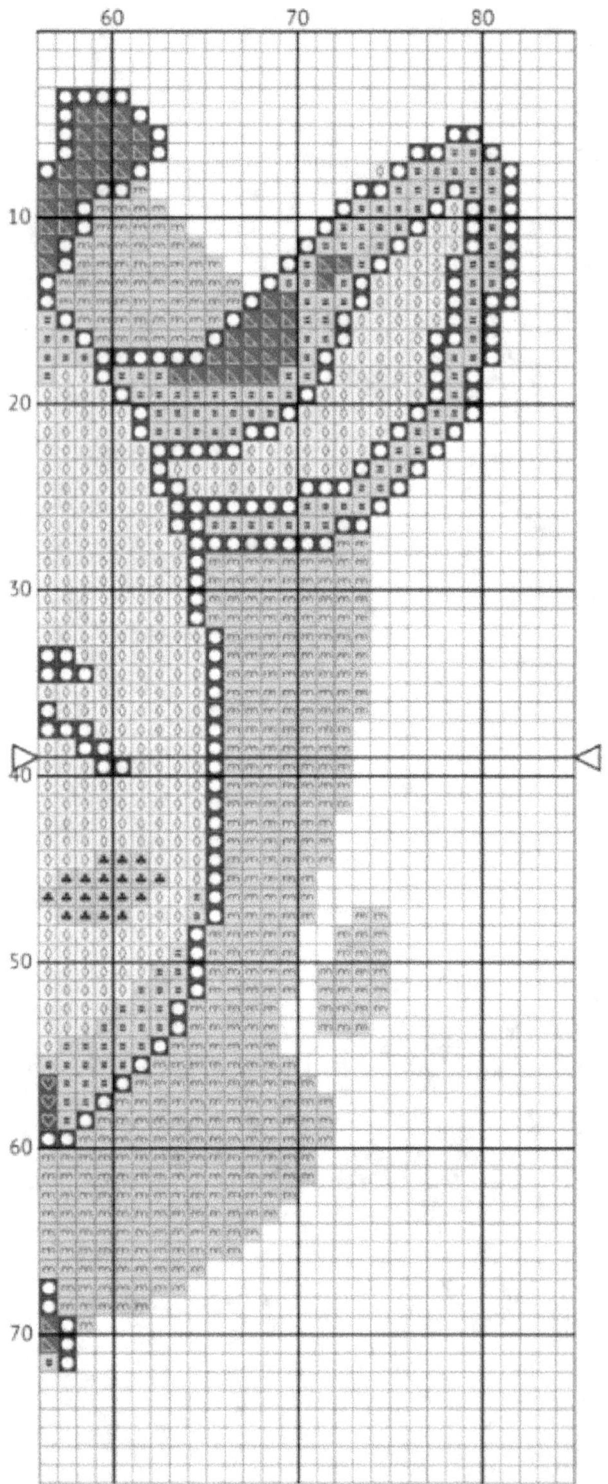

Koala / Koala

Design size: 85 x 71 stitches

Floss list for crosses

Use 2 strands of thread for cross stitch

N	Symbol		Number	Name	Stitches
1	◯	◯	DMC B5200	Snow White	72
2	=	=	DMC 02	Tin	293
3	♣	♣	DMC 30	Blueberry - Medium Light	214
4	m	m	DMC 160	Gray Blue - Medium	1625
5	◺	◺	DMC 336	Navy Blue	536
6	◇	◇	DMC 963	Dusty Rose - Ultra Very Light	567
7	●	●	DMC 3753	Antique Blue - Ultra Very Light	480

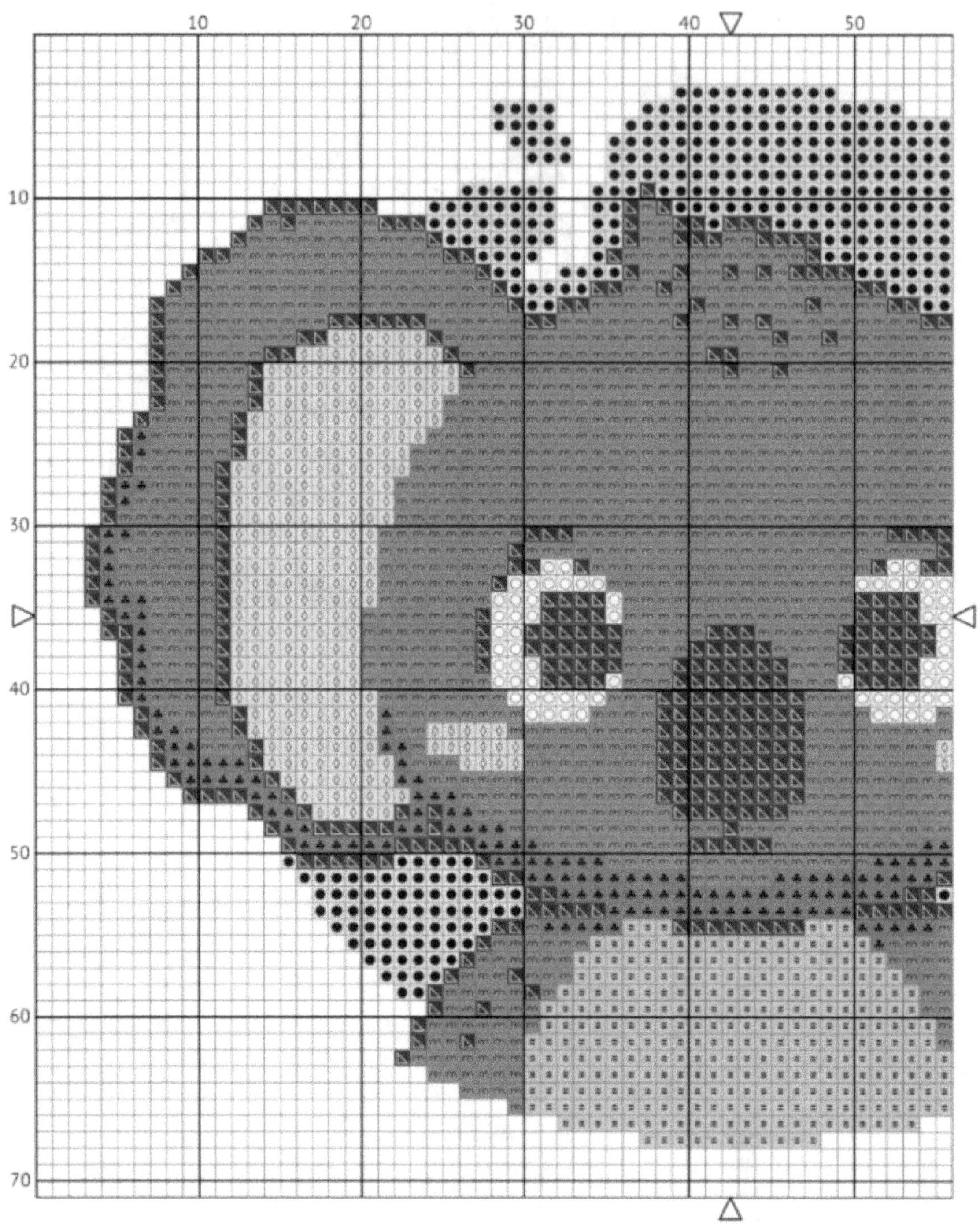

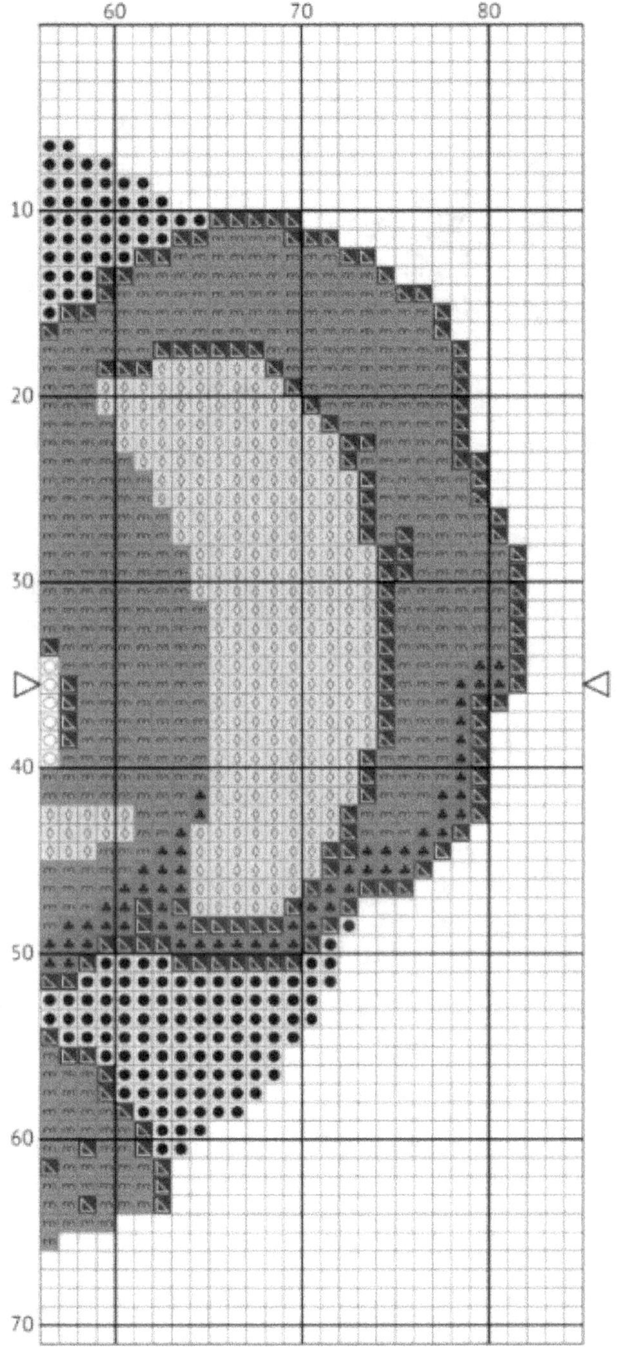

Lion / León

Design size: 85 x 84 stitches

Floss list for crosses

Use 2 strands of thread for cross stitch

N	Symbol		Number	Name	Stitches
1	Γ	Γ	DMC B5200	Snow White	67
2	◊	◊	DMC 19	Autumn Gold - Medium Light	1160
3	m	m	DMC 22	Alizarin	1374
4	✕	✕	DMC 746	Off White	646
5	☆	☆	DMC 902	Garnet - Very Dark	515
6	♣	♣	DMC 957	Geranium - Pale	35
7	▽	▽	DMC 3777	Terra Cotta - Very Dark	81
8	♡	♡	DMC 3779	Rosewood - Very Light	748

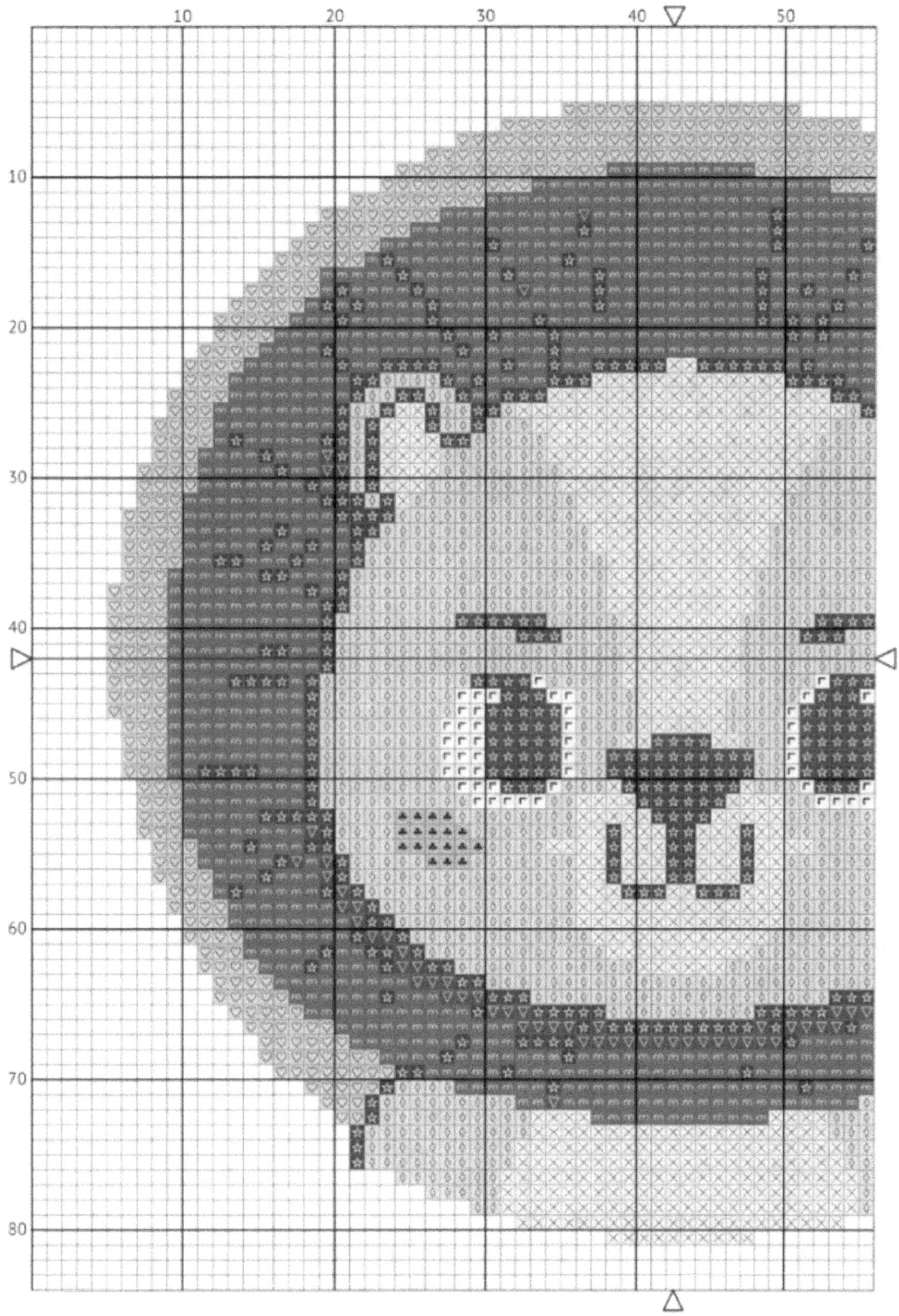

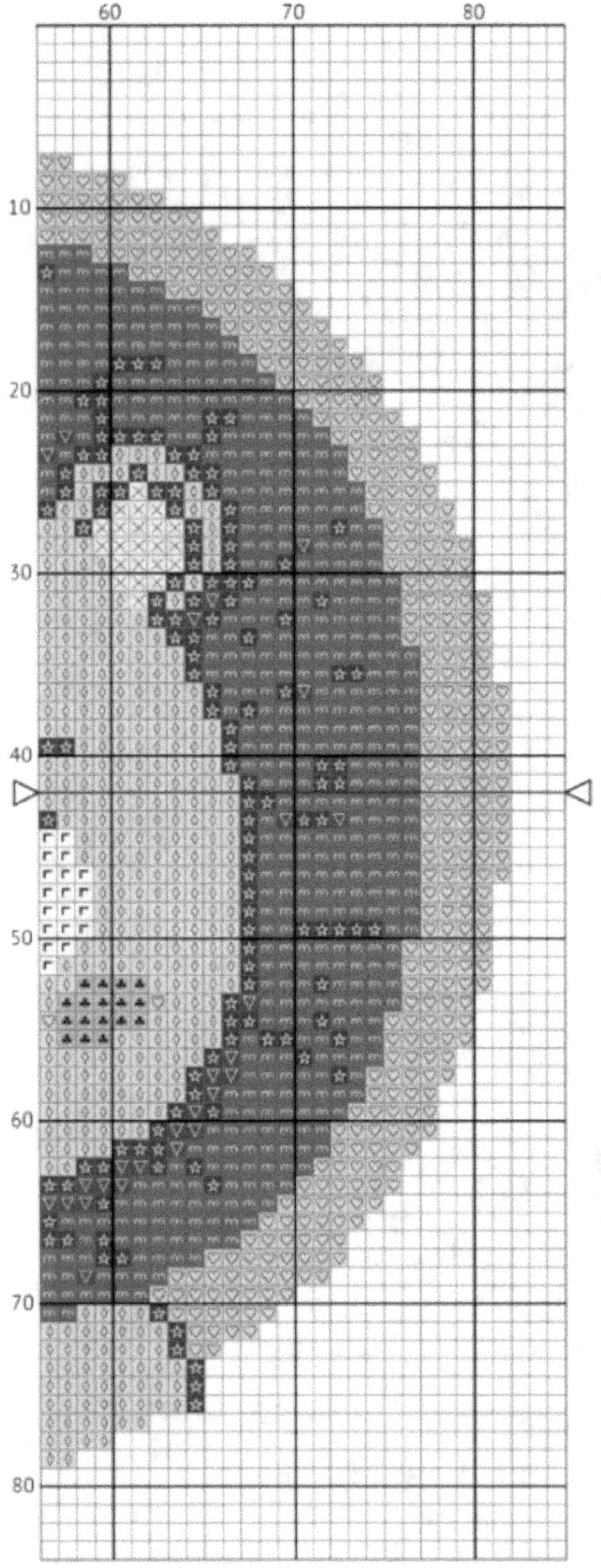

Chimpanzee / Chimpancé

Design size: 85 × 82 stitches

Floss list for crosses

Use 2 strands of thread for cross stitch

N	Symbol		Number	Name	Stitches
1	♡	♡	DMC 22	Alizarin	684
2	=	=	DMC 434	Brown - Light	9
3	♣	♣	DMC 451	Shell Gray - Dark	2
4	☆	☆	DMC 758	Terra Cotta - Very Light	29
5	◣	◣	DMC 814	Garnet - Dark	370
6	○	○	DMC 950	Desert Sand - Light	1416
7	◇	◇	DMC 3689	Mauve - Light	26
8	●	●	DMC 3747	Blue Violet - Very Light	715
9	▽	▽	DMC 3856	Mahogany - Ultra Very Light	1

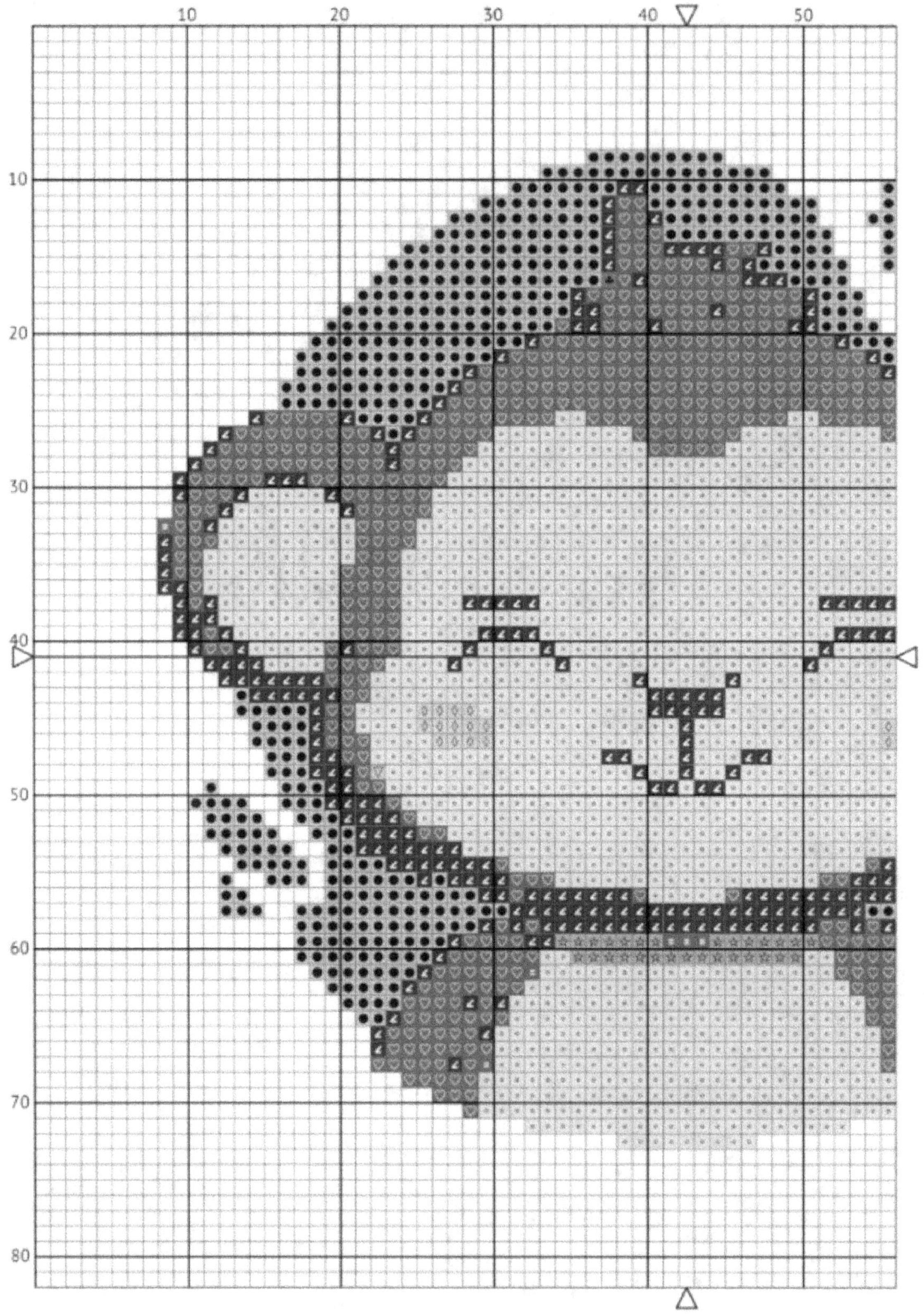

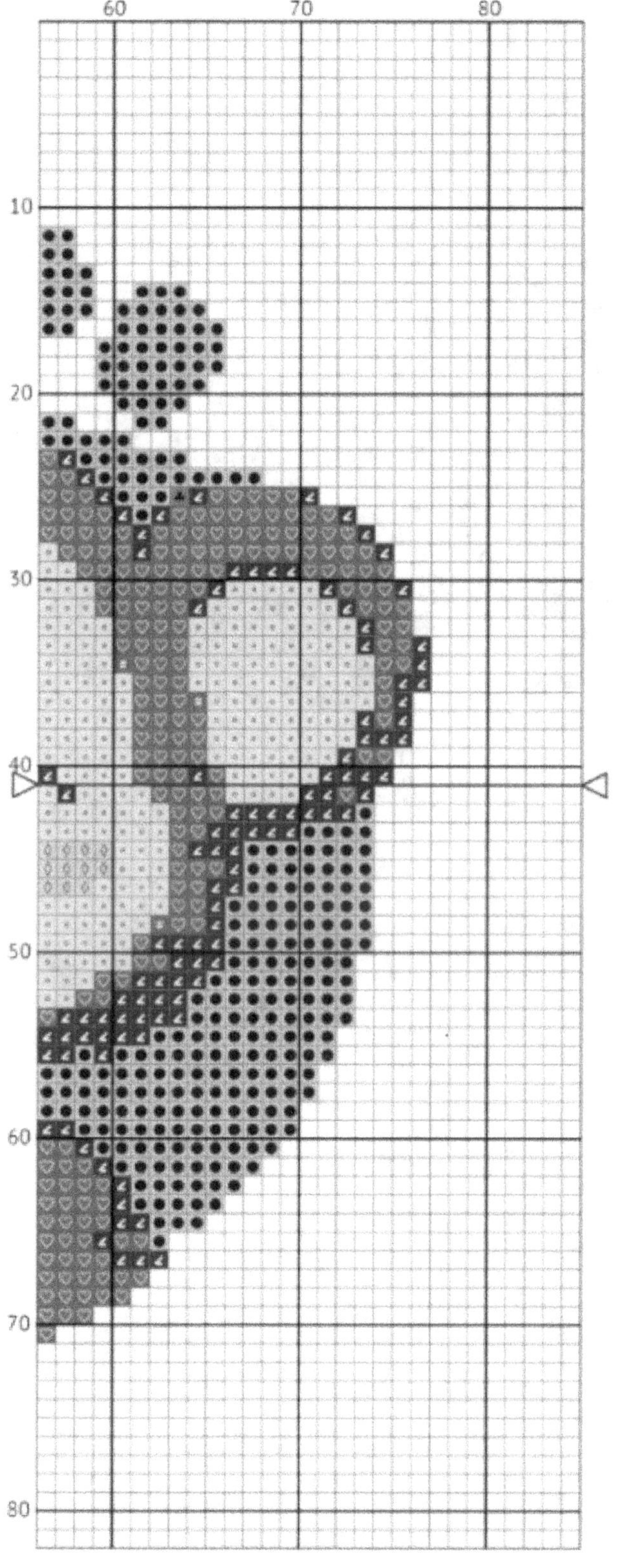

Lazy / Perezoso

Design size: 85 x 80 stitches

Floss list for crosses

Use 2 strands of thread for cross stitch

N	Symbol		Number	Name	Stitches
1	◊	◊	DMC B5200	Snow White	38
2	♣	♣	DMC 402	Mahogany - Very Light	106
3	♡	♡	DMC 758	Terra Cotta - Very Light	469
4	◣	◣	DMC 918	Red Copper - Dark	254
5	✿	✿	DMC 951	Tawny - Light	831
6	●	●	DMC 955	Nile Green - Light	901
7	■	■	DMC 967	Apricot - Very Light	59
8	∘	∘	DMC 3856	Mahogany - Ultra Very Light	30
9	m	m	DMC 3859	Rosewood - Light	216

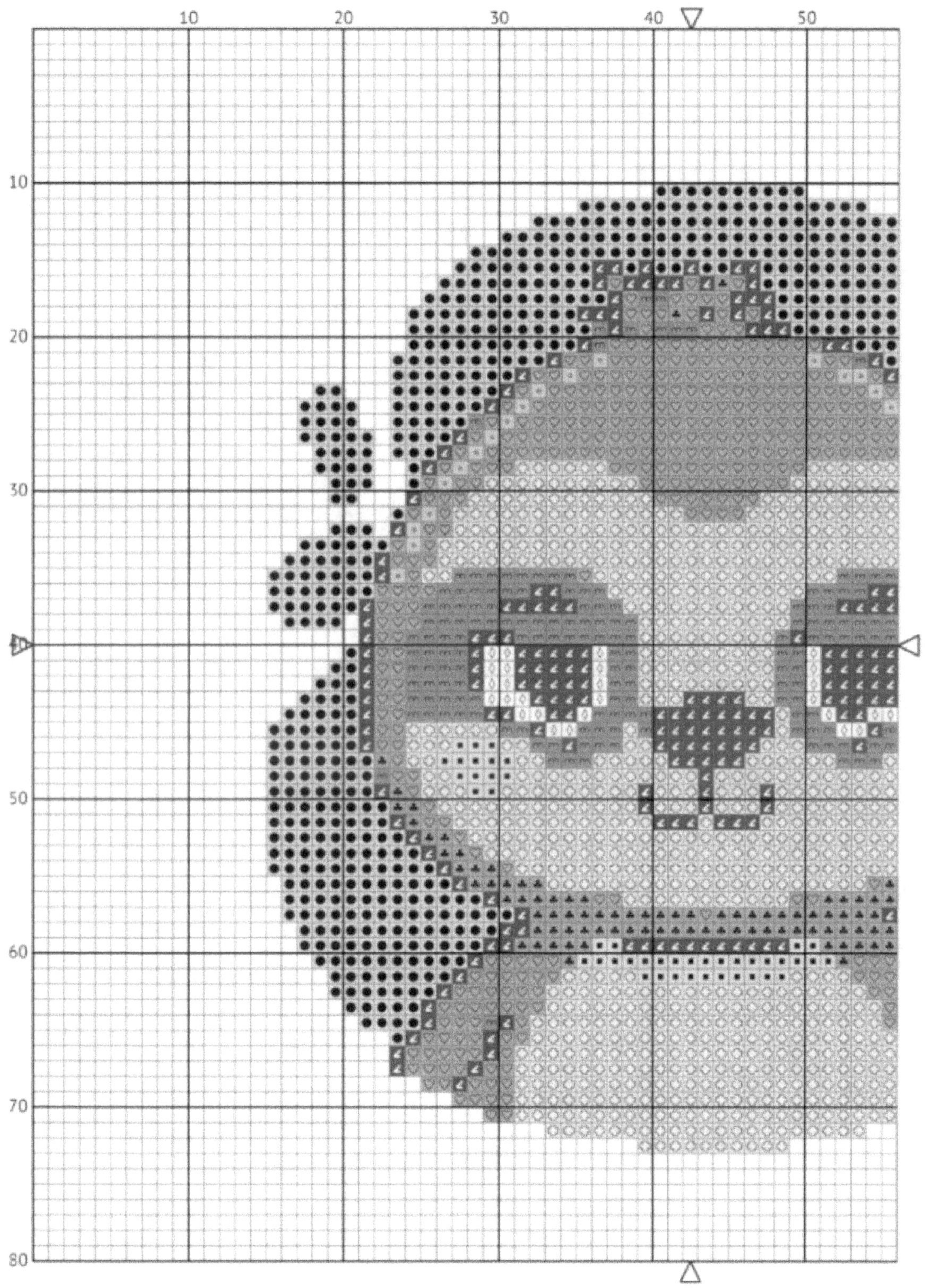

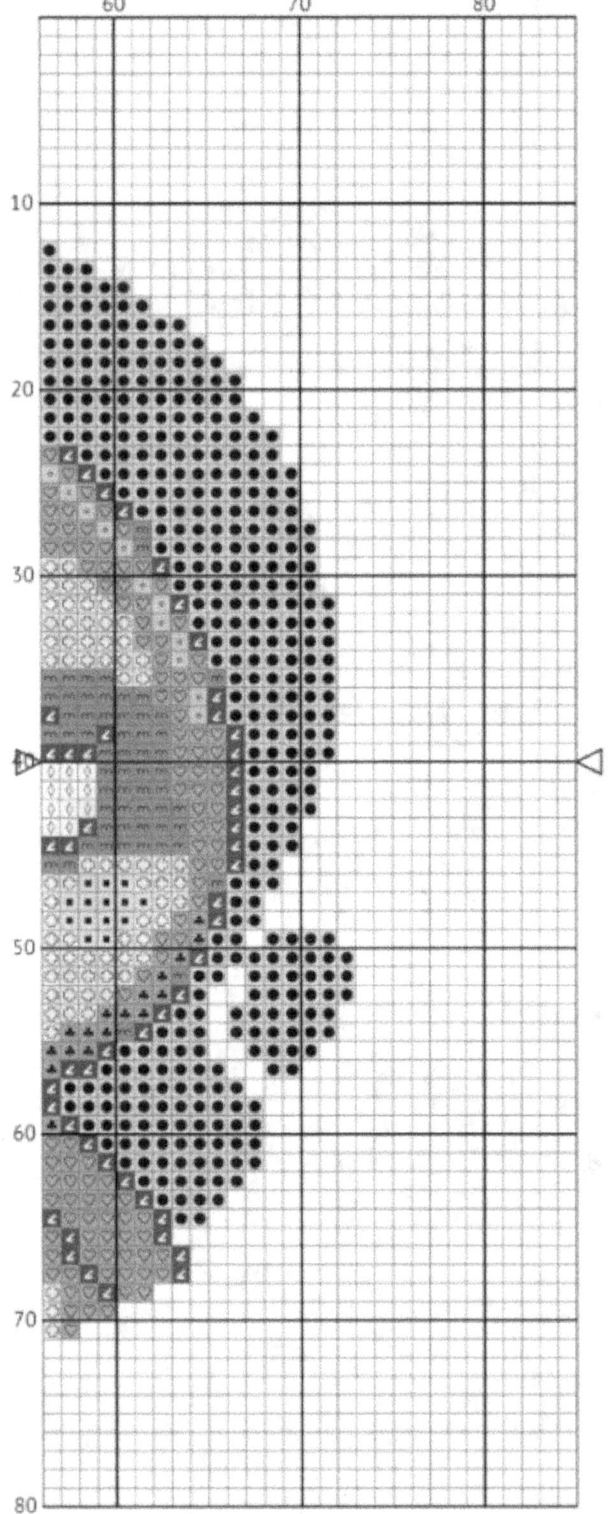

Seal / Foca

Design size: 85 x 81 stitches

Floss list for crosses

Use 2 strands of thread for cross stitch

N	Symbol	Number	Name	Stitches
1		DMC B5200	Snow White	54
2		DMC 24	Lavender - White	1280
3		DMC 210	Lavender - Medium	17
4		DMC 211	Lavender - Light	289
5		DMC 225	Shell Pink - Ultra Very Light	161
6		DMC 552	Violet - Medium	311
7		DMC 745	Yellow - Light Pale	1059
8		DMC 945	Tawny	1

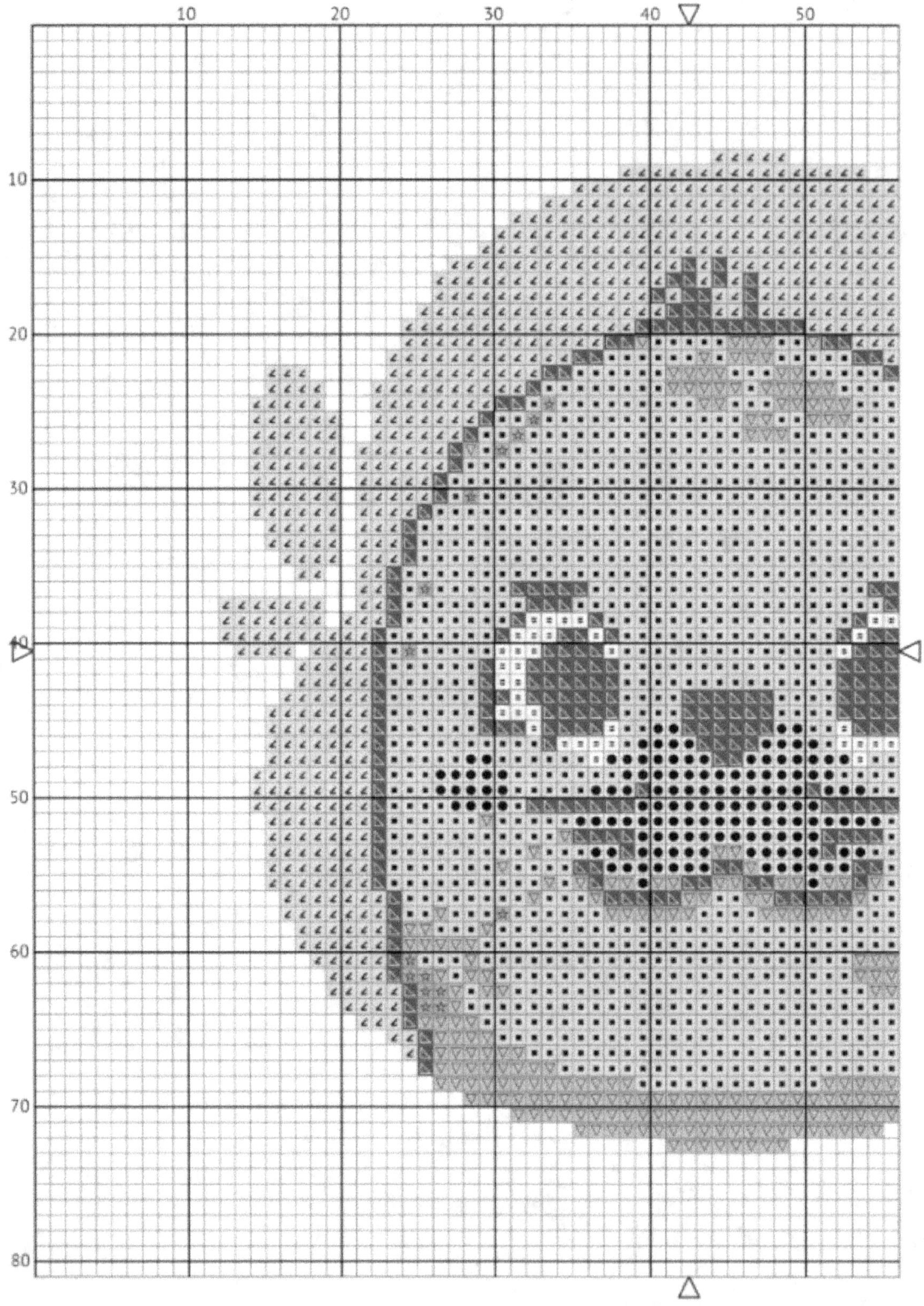

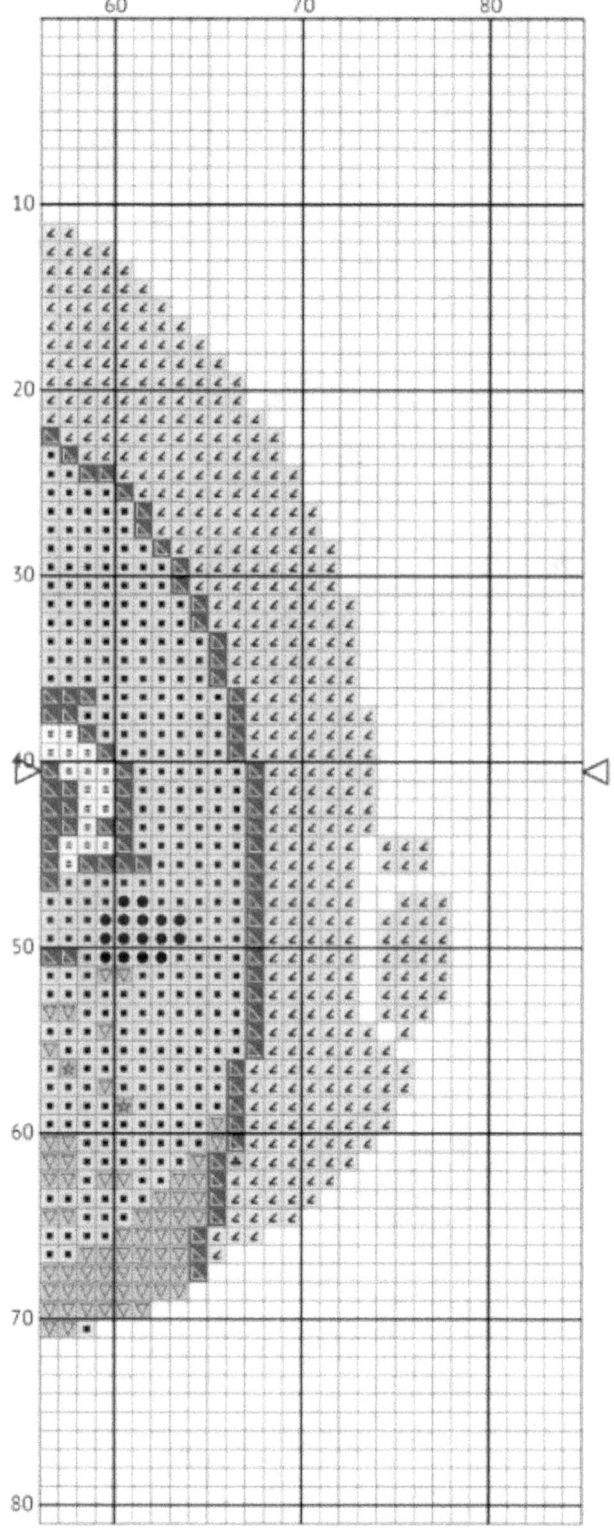

Walrus / Morsal

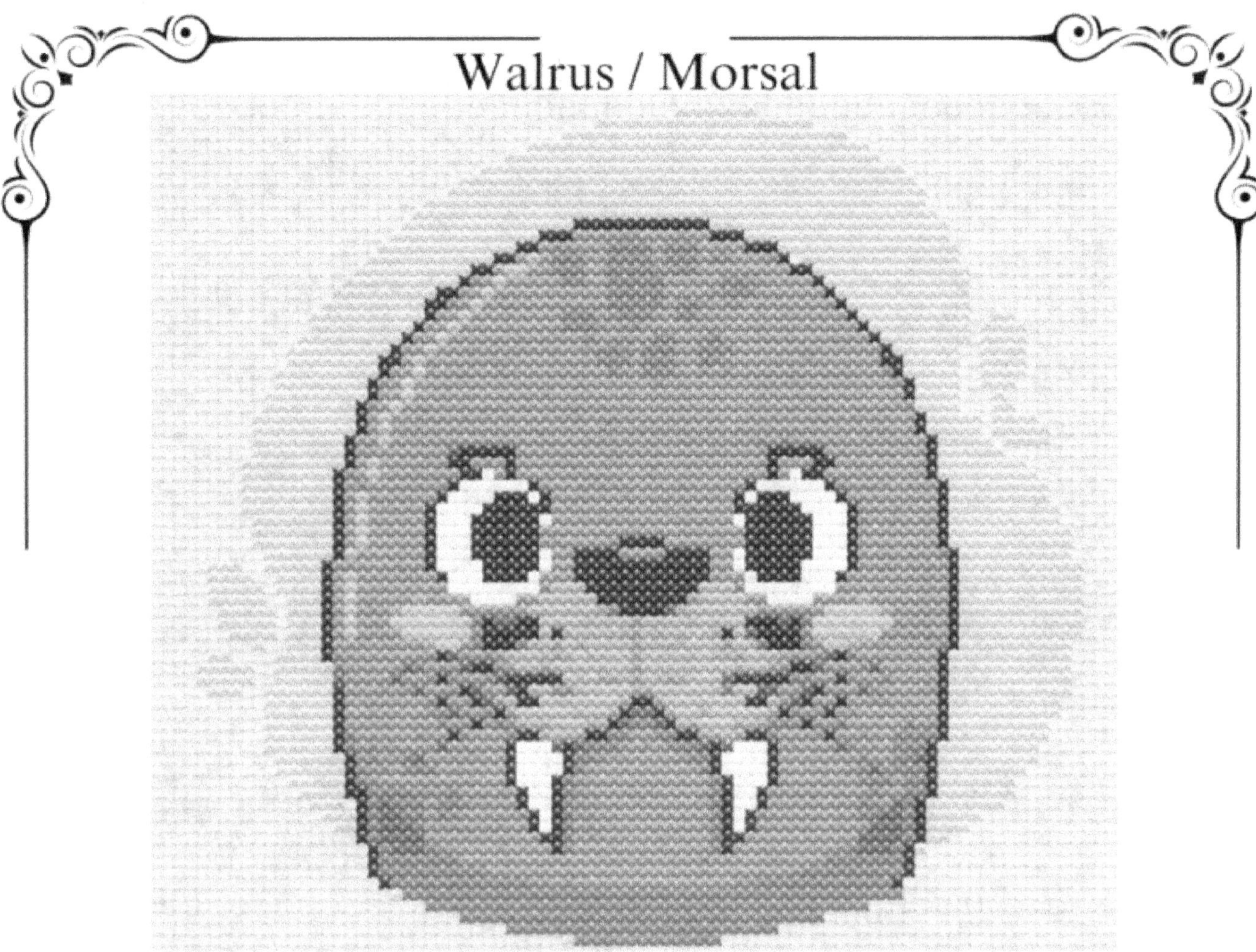

Floss list for crosses

Design size: 85 x 77 stitches

Use 2 strands of thread for cross stitch

N	Symbol		Number	Name	Stitches
1	○	○	DMC B5200	Snow White	142
2	=	=	DMC 06	Driftwood - Medium Light	157
3	⌐	⌐	DMC 152	Shell Pink - Medium Light	38
4	■	■	DMC 167	Yellow Beige - Very Dark	407
5	○	○	DMC 407	Desert Sand - Dark	1516
6	m	m	DMC 435	Brown - Very Light	65
7	✕	✕	DMC 543	Beige - Ultra Very Light	32
8	◹	◹	DMC 801	Coffee Brown - Dark	438
9	◢	◢	DMC 955	Nile Green - Light	1298
10	❖	❖	DMC 3064	Desert Sand	111
11	‹	‹	DMC 3689	Mauve - Light	40
12	◊	◊	DMC 3864	Mocha Beige - Light	40
13	✳	✳	DMC 3866	Mocha - Ultra Very Light	2

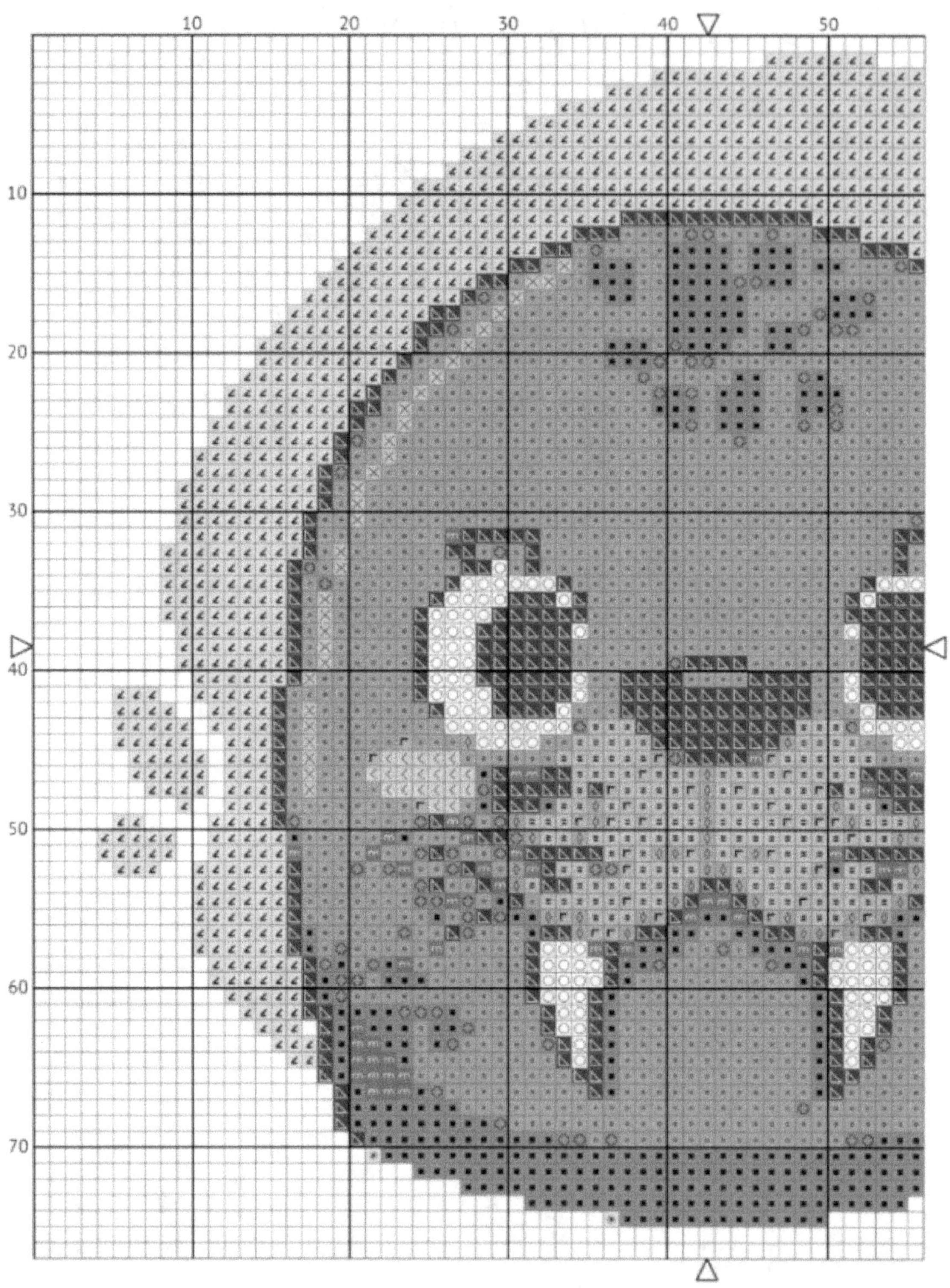

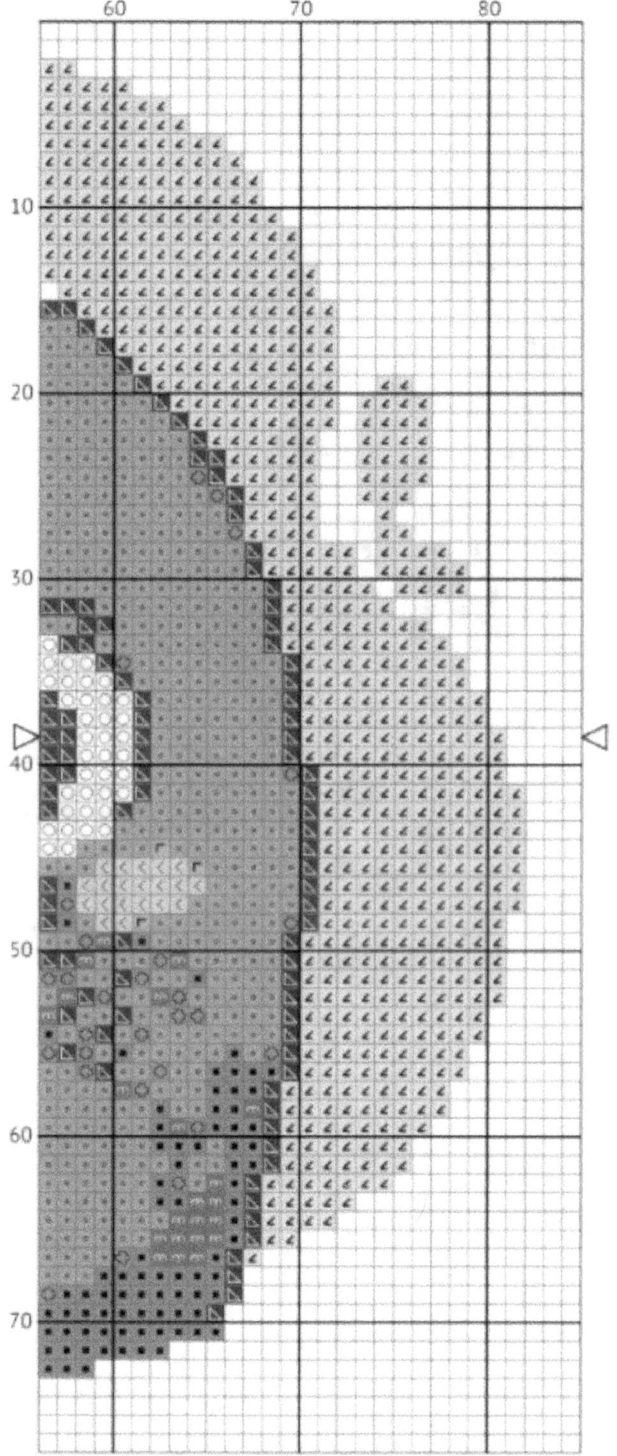

Lemur / Lemur

Design size: 85 x 84 stitches

Floss list for crosses

Use 2 strands of thread for cross stitch

N	Symbol		Number	Name	Stitches
1	◊	◊	DMC B5200	Snow White	94
2	◺	◪	DMC 04	Tin - Dark	1228
3	◿	◺	DMC 09	Cocoa - Very Dark	704
4	●	●	DMC 14	Apple Green - Pale	1308
5	m	m	DMC 3713	Salmon - Very Light	40
6	✤	✤	DMC 3774	Desert Sand - Very Light	1006

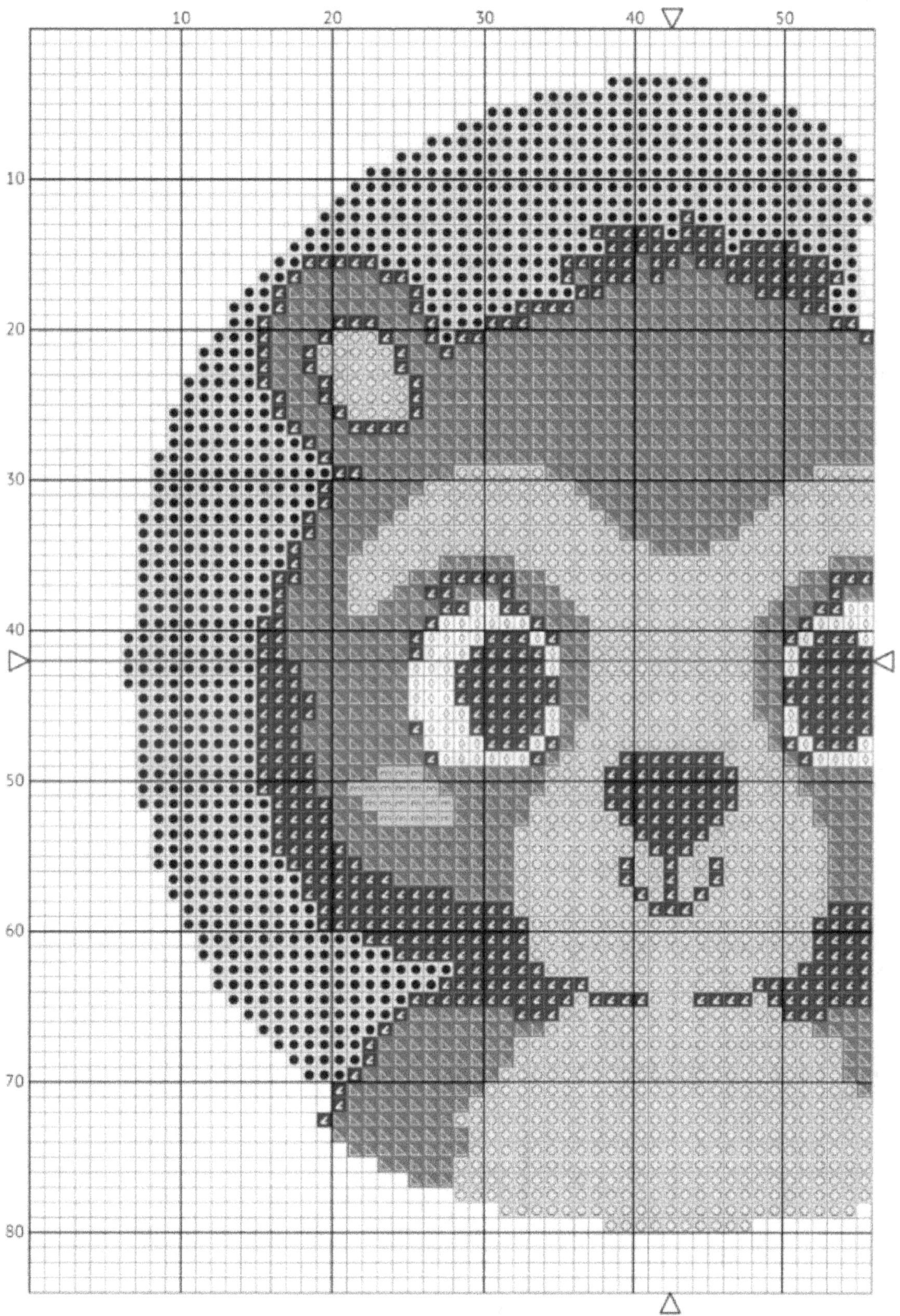

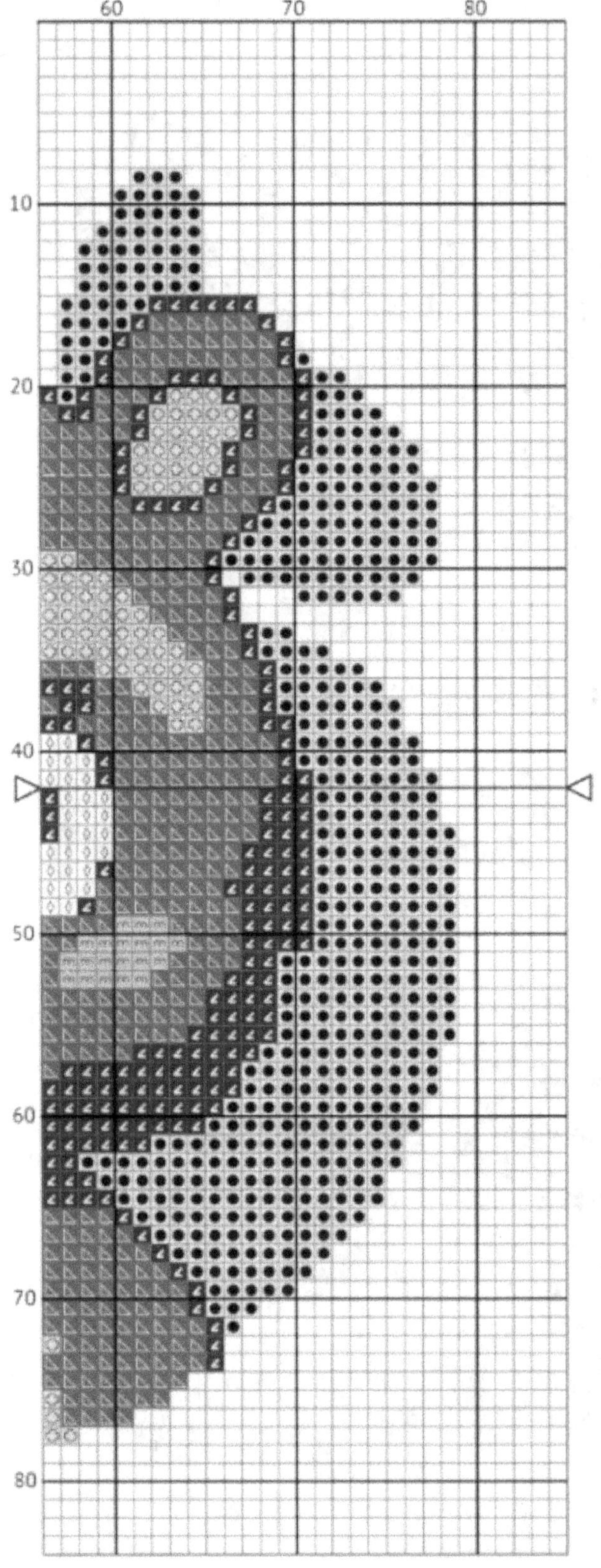

Bear / Oso

Design size: 85 x 82 stitches

Floss list for crosses

Use 2 strands of thread for cross stitch

N	Symbol		Number	Name	Stitches
1	▽	▽	DMC B5200	Snow White	74
2	◣	◣	DMC 19	Autumn Gold - Medium Light	1353
3	♣	♣	DMC 221	Shell Pink - Very Dark	235
4	m	m	DMC 356	Terra Cotta - Medium	499
5	♡	♥	DMC 814	Garnet - Dark	514
6	◹	◹	DMC 3721	Shell Pink - Dark	1800

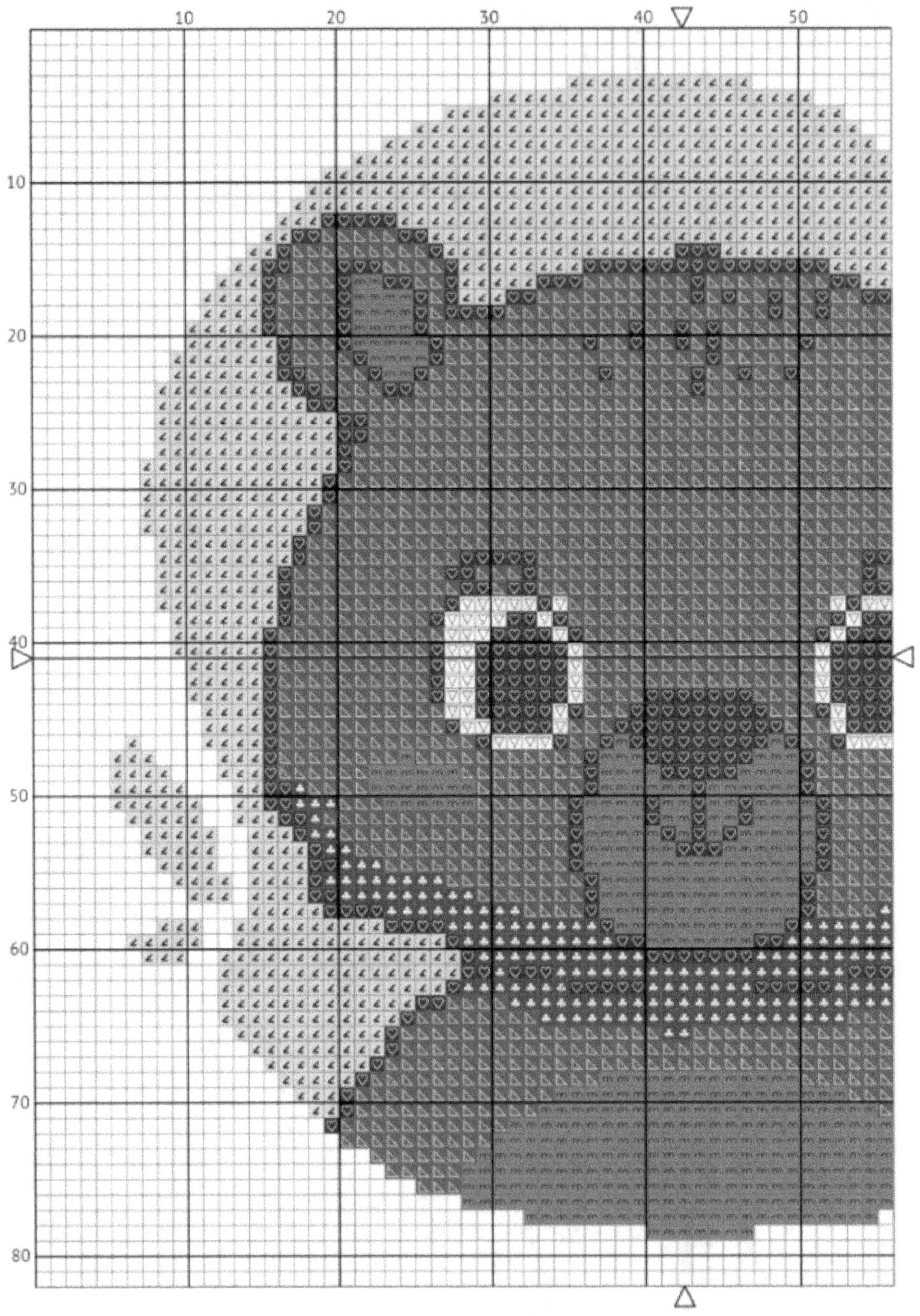

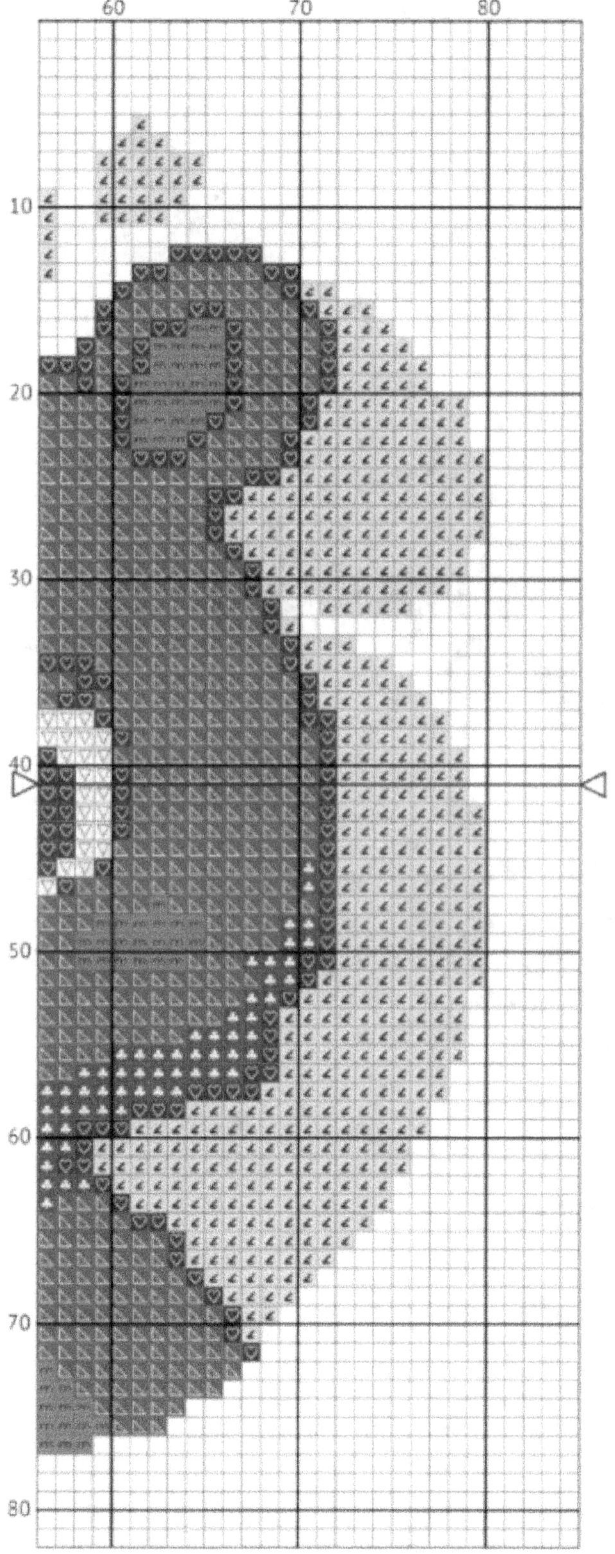

Panda / Panda

Design size: 85 x 87 stitches

Floss list for crosses

Use 2 strands of thread for cross stitch

N	Symbol		Number	Name	Stitches
1	☆	★	DMC 30	Blueberry - Medium Light	146
2	◺	◺	DMC 336	Navy Blue	611
3	○	○	DMC 3753	Antique Blue - Ultra Very Light	177
4	✛	✛	DMC 3807	Cornflower Blue	1423
5	♡	♡	DMC BLANK	White	1486
6	∠	∠	DMC 3689	Mauve - Light	1457

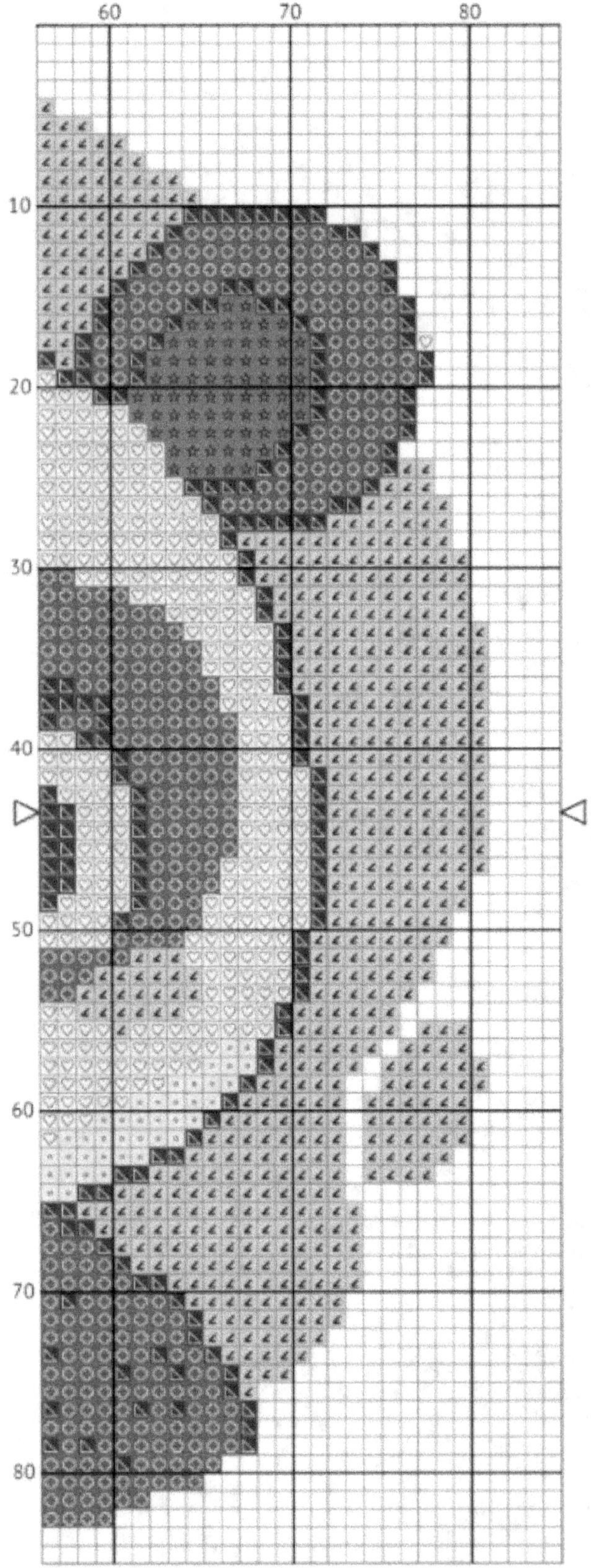

Polar Bear / Oso Polar

Design size: 85 x 86 stitches

Floss list for crosses

Use 2 strands of thread for cross stitch

N	Symbol		Number	Name	Stitches
1	☆	☆	DMC B5200	Snow White	232
2	○	○	DMC 25	Lavender - Ultra Light	205
3	♡	♡	DMC 161	Gray Blue	365
4	∠	∠	DMC 162	Blue - Ultra Very Light	1729
5	✿	✿	DMC 3779	Rosewood - Very Light	40
6	●	●	DMC BLANK	White	2272

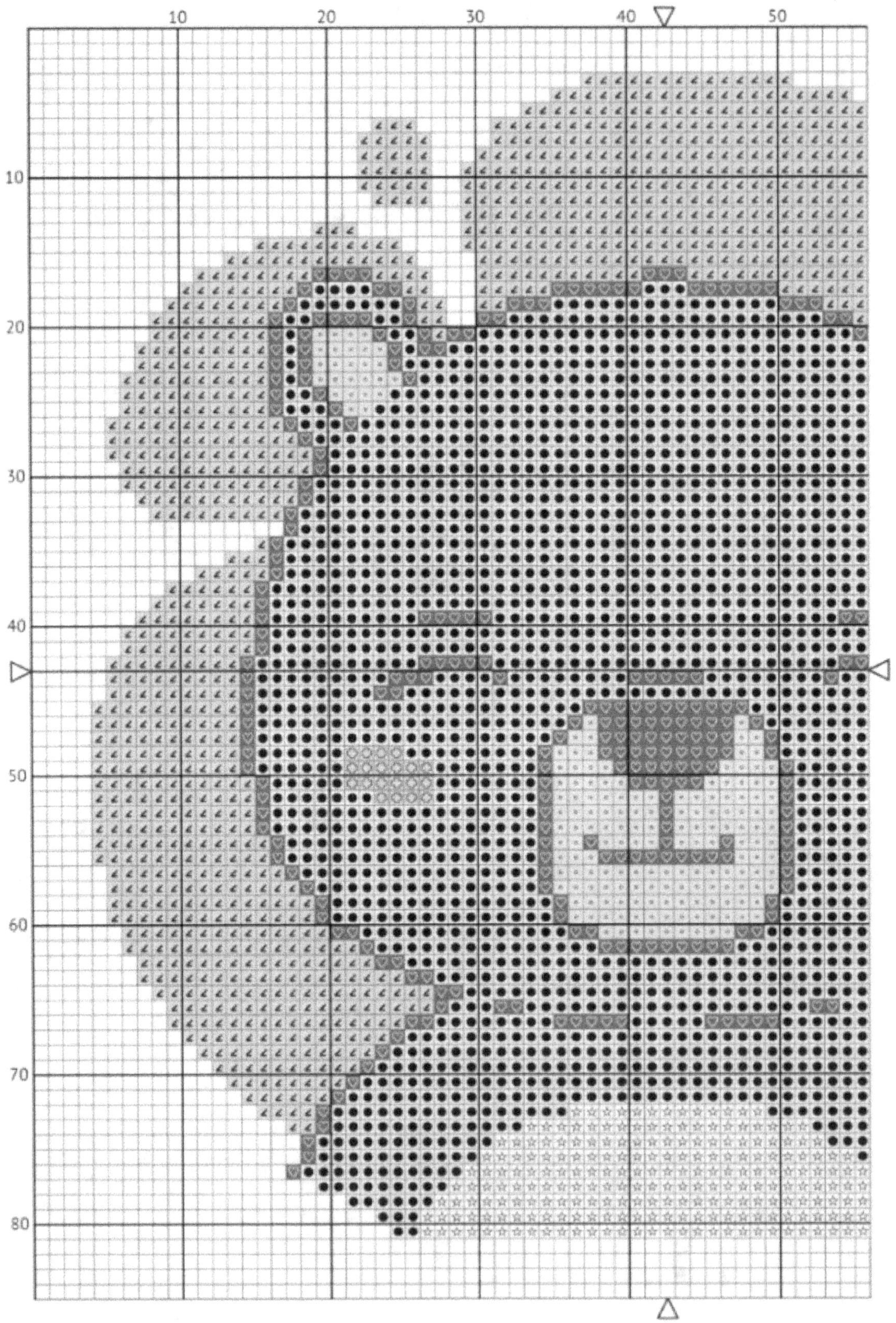

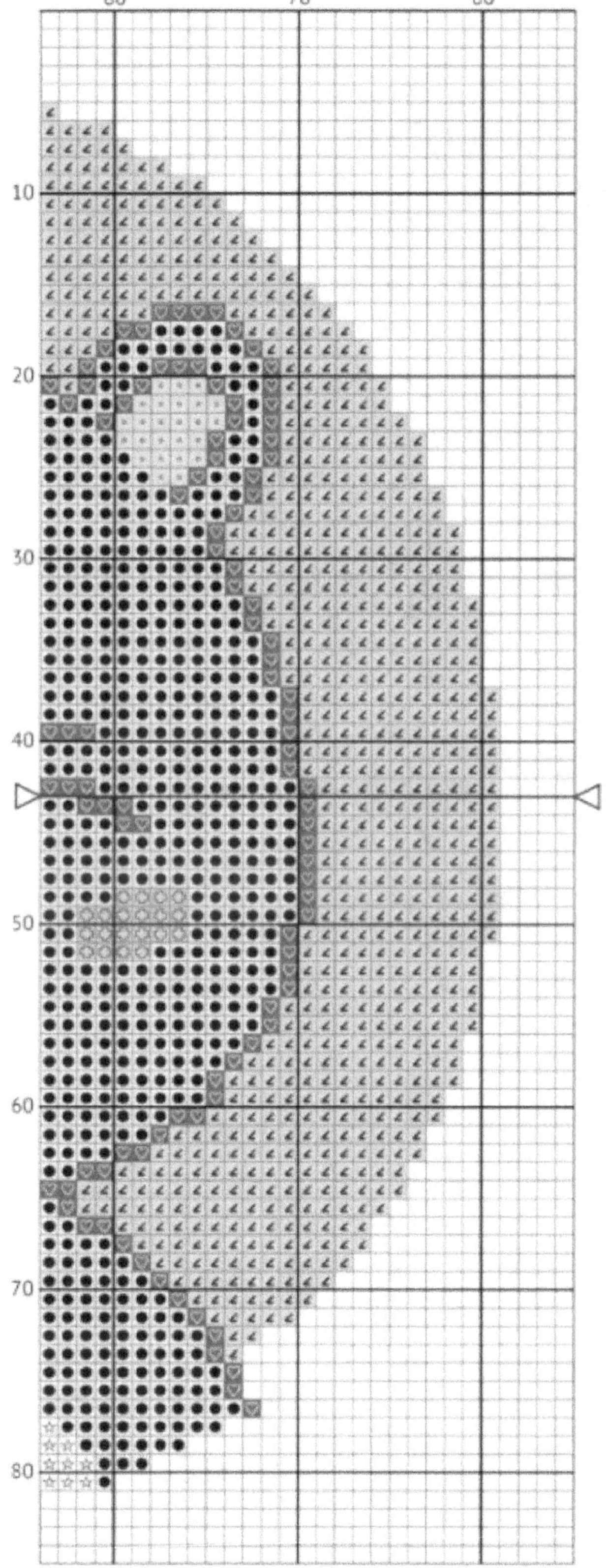

Sheep / Oveja

Design size: 85 x 82 stitches

Floss list for crosses

Use 2 strands of thread for cross stitch

N	Symbol		Number	Name	Stitches
1	◊	◊	DMC B5200	Snow White	100
2	■	■	DMC 210	Lavender - Medium	110
3	☆	☆	DMC 444	Lemon - Dark	48
4	●	●	DMC 746	Off White	676
5	m	m	DMC 918	Red Copper - Dark	526
6	♡	♡	DMC 957	Geranium - Pale	1666
7	∠	∠	DMC 3774	Desert Sand - Very Light	1476

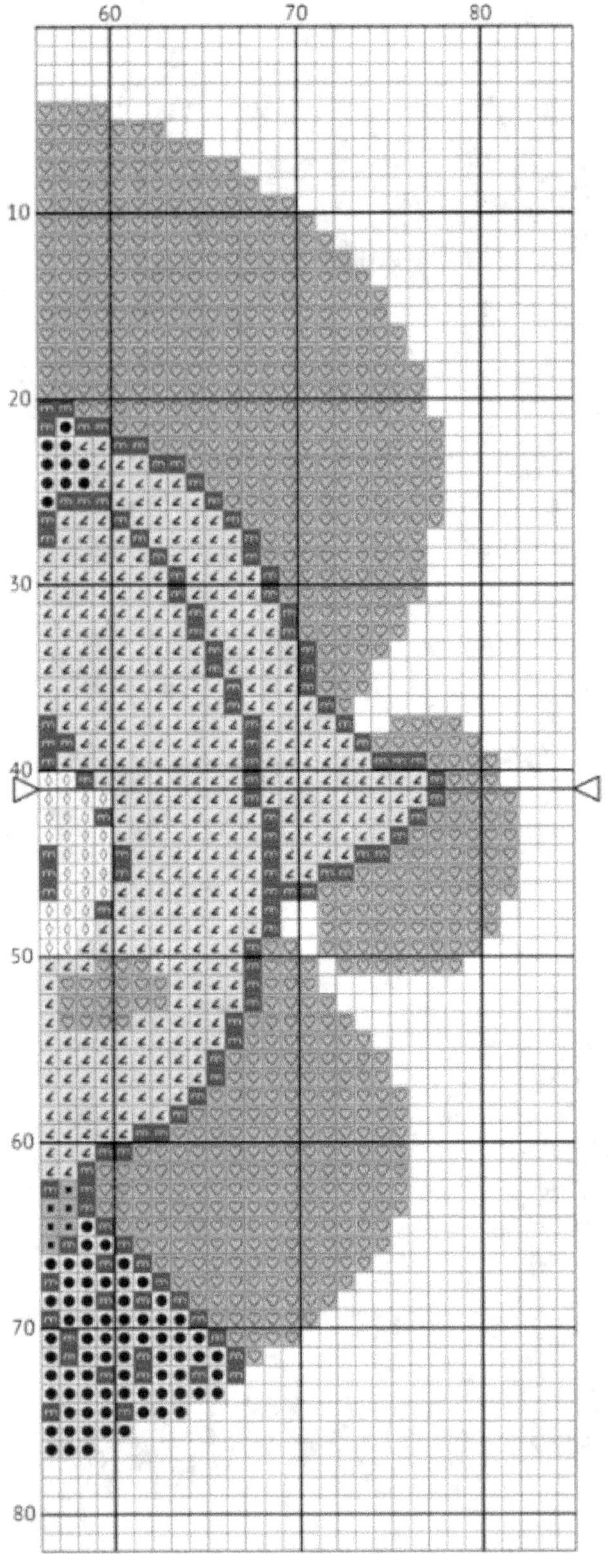

Marsupial / Marsupial

Design size: 85 x 87 stitches

Use 2 strands of thread for cross stitch

N	Symbol		Number	Name	Stitches
1	▽	▽	DMC B5200	Snow White	115
2	●	●	DMC 225	Shell Pink - Ultra Very Light	537
3	∠	∠	DMC 353	Peach	178
4	m	m	DMC 437	Tan - Light	510
5	◿	◿	DMC 814	Garnet - Dark	652
6	✛	✛	DMC 950	Desert Sand - Light	1010
7	■	■	DMC 967	Apricot - Very Light	25
8	♡	♡	DMC 3708	Melon - Light	1457
9	♣	♣	DMC 3777	Terra Cotta - Very Dark	409

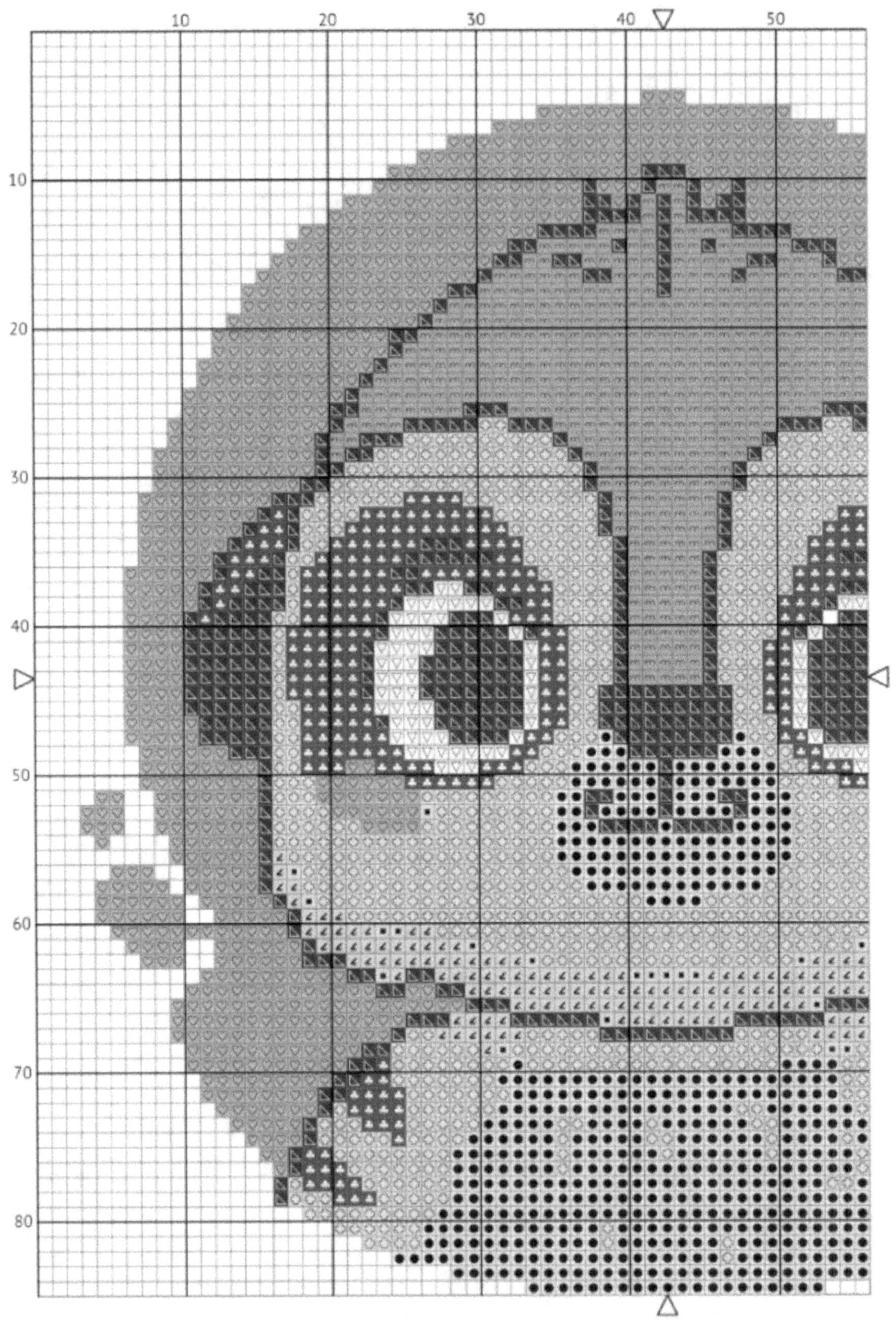

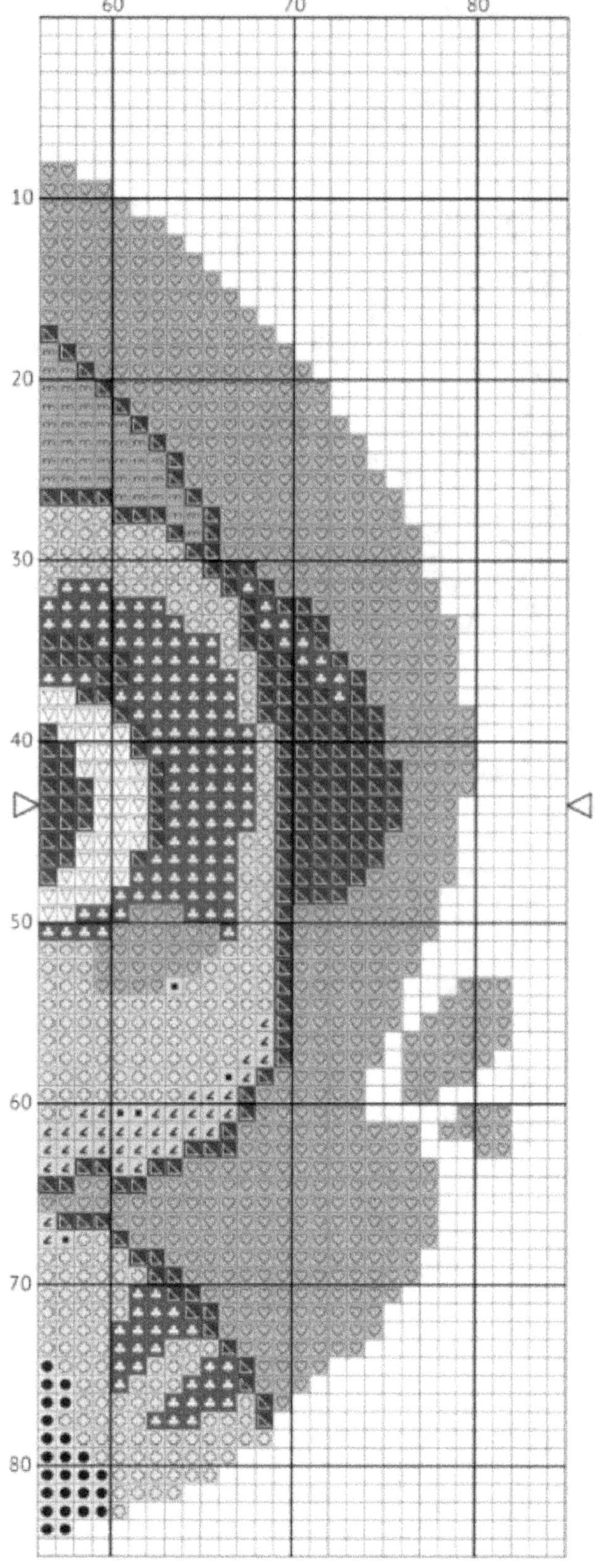

Penguin / Pingüino

Design size: 85 x 79 stitches

Floss list for crosses

Use 2 strands of thread for cross stitch

N	Symbol		Number	Name	Stitches
1	♣	♣	DMC 32	Blueberry - Dark	103
2	■	■	DMC 168	Pewter - Very Light	115
3	♡	♡	DMC 336	Navy Blue	328
4	⌐	⌐	DMC 3779	Rosewood - Very Light	46
5	m	m	DMC 3807	Cornflower Blue	703
6	∠	∠	DMC BLANK	White	1388
7	●	●	DMC 747	Sky Blue - Very Light	1624
8	◊	◊	DMC 3827	Golden Brown - Pale	54

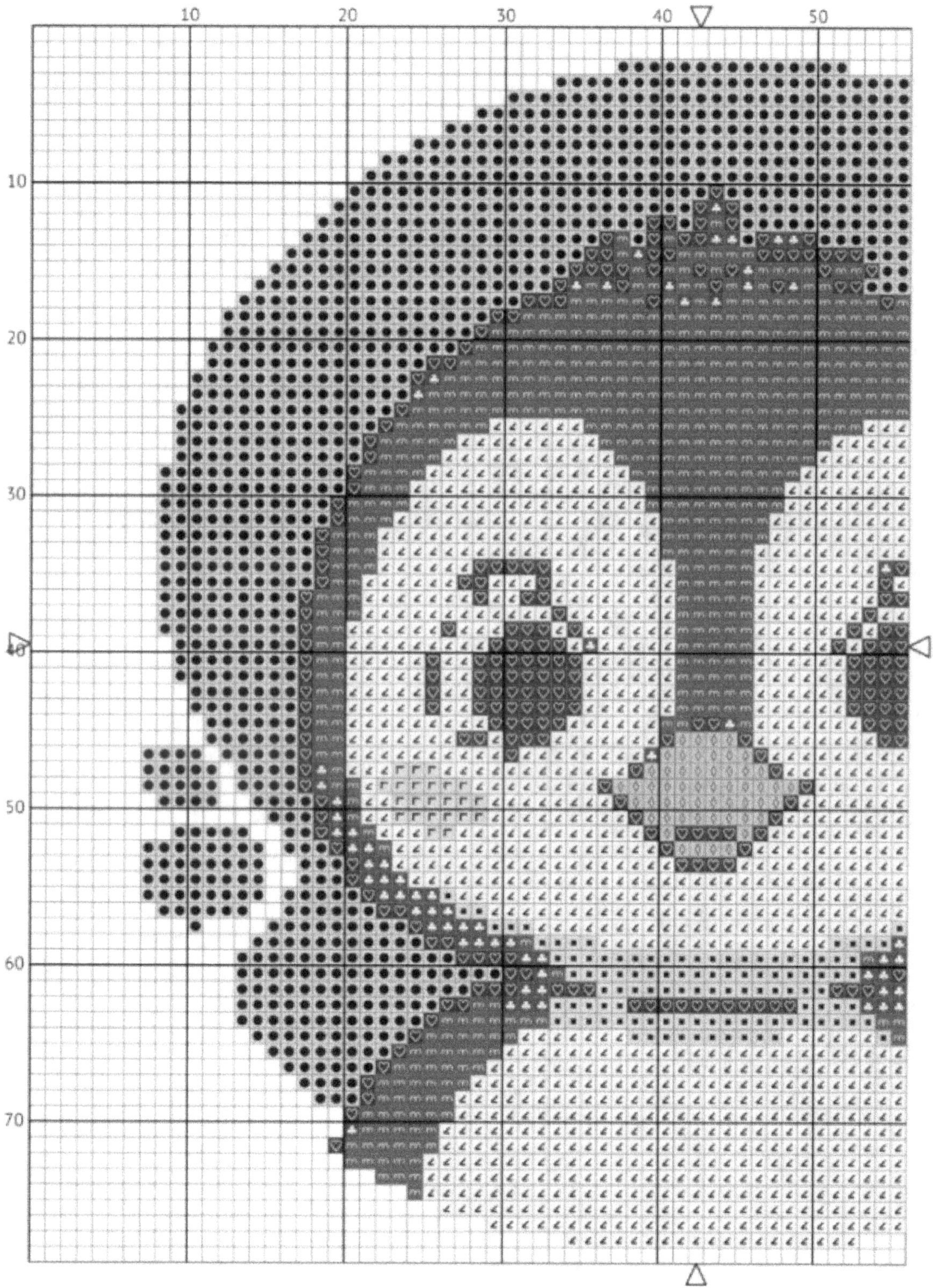

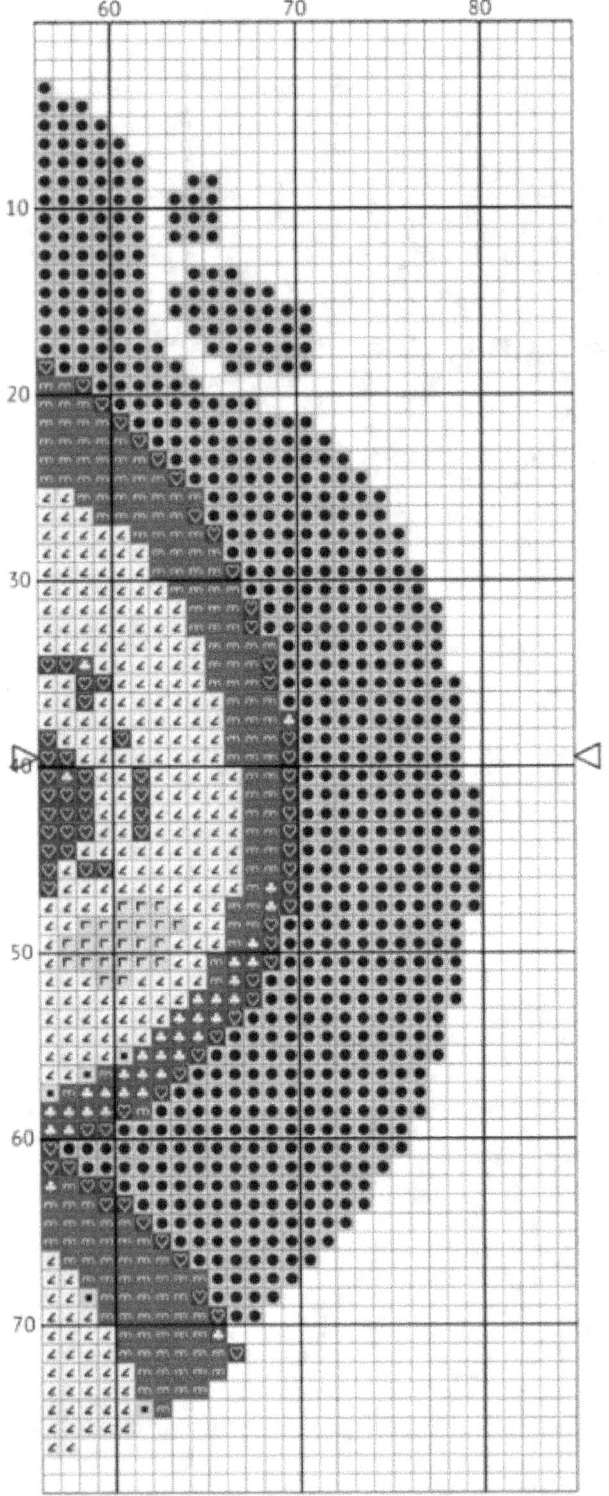

Chick / Pollito

Design size: 85 x 87 stitches

Floss list for crosses

Use 2 strands of thread for cross stitch

N	Symbol		Number	Name	Stitches
1	☆	☆	DMC B5200	Snow White	94
2	■	■	DMC 19	Autumn Gold - Medium Light	296
3	◺	◺	DMC 745	Yellow - Light Pale	2321
4	●	●	DMC 775	Baby Blue - Very Light	1537
5	▽	▽	DMC 3326	Rose - Light	38
6	◤	◤	DMC 3721	Shell Pink - Dark	454
7	♣	♣	DMC 3827	Golden Brown - Pale	153

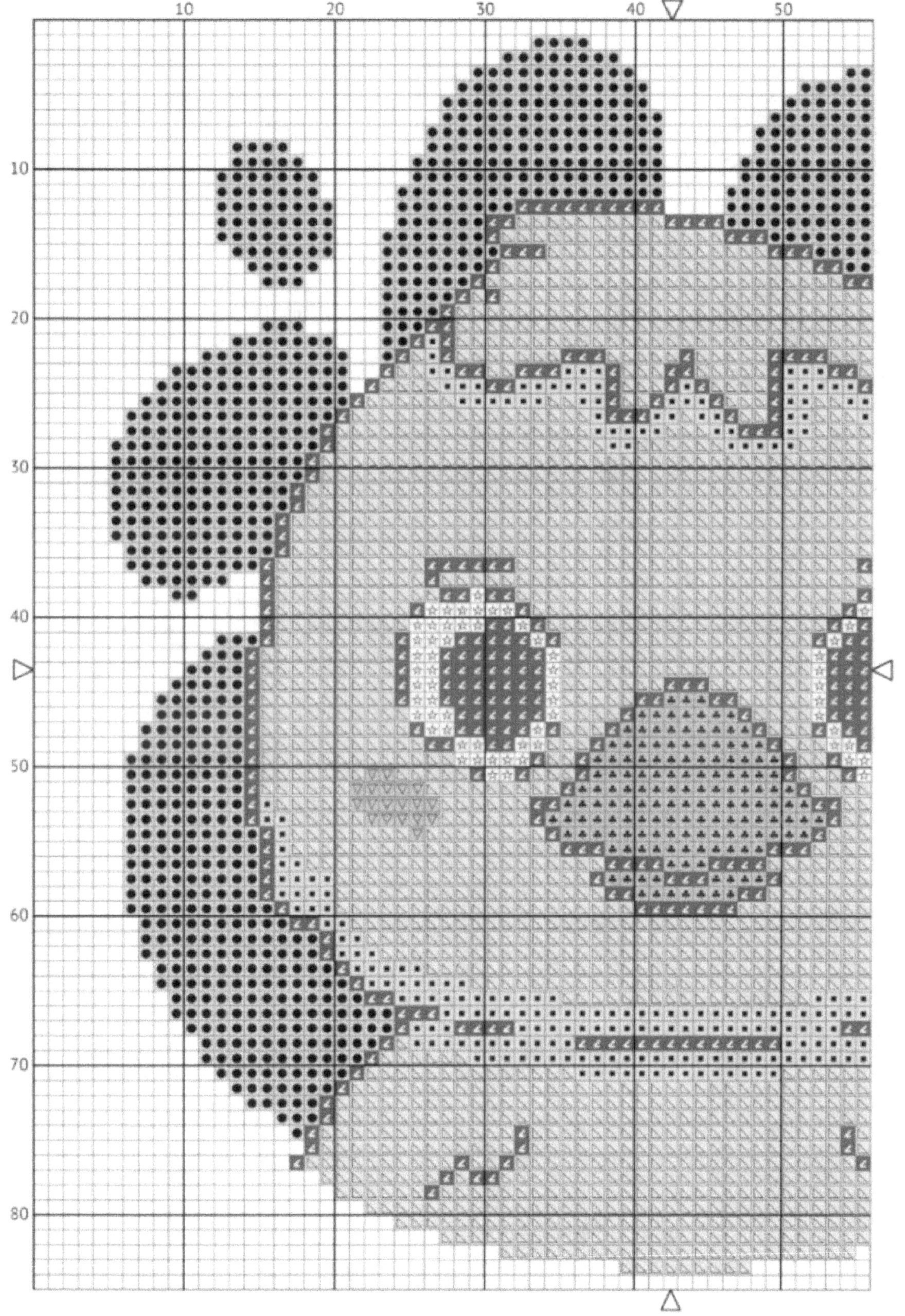

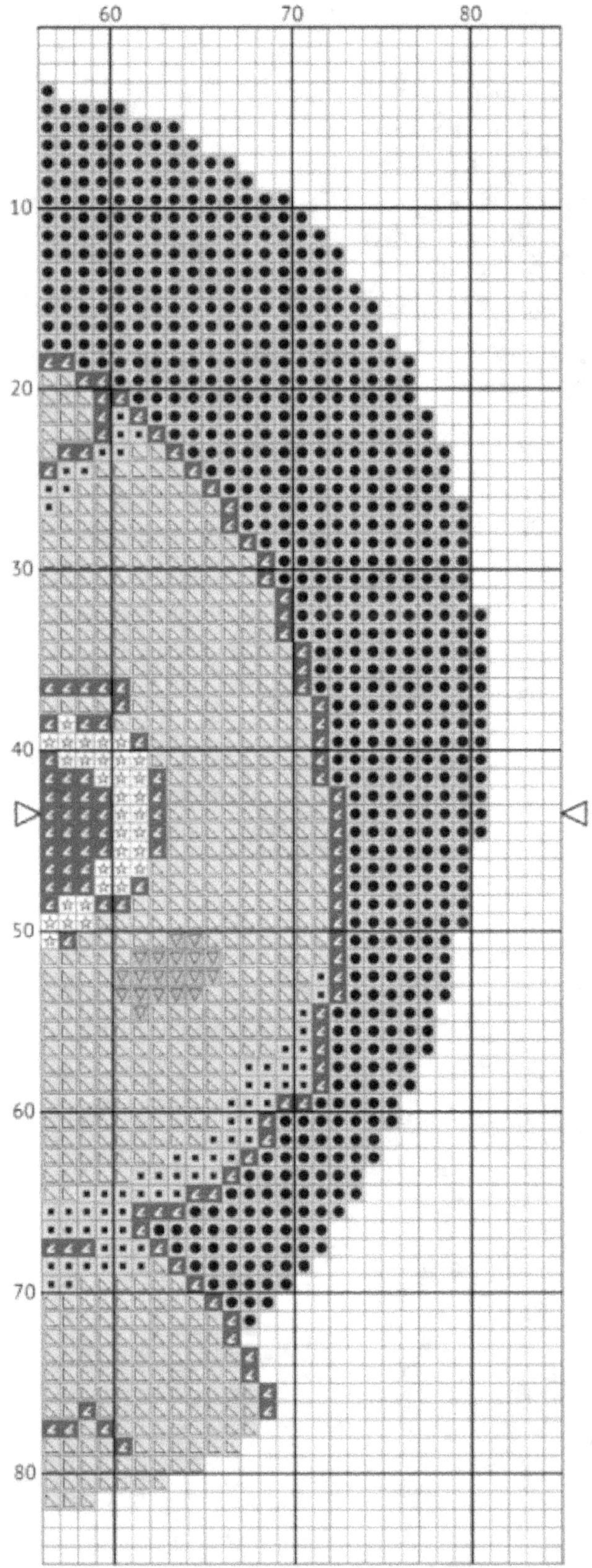

Reindeer / Reno

Floss list for crosses

Use 2 strands of thread for cross stitch

N	Symbol		Number	Name	Stitches
1	◊	◊	DMC B5200	Snow White	85
2	◺	◺	DMC 353	Peach	27
3	◣	◣	DMC 355	Terra Cotta - Dark	417
4	●	●	DMC 356	Terra Cotta - Medium	242
5	▽	▽	DMC 740	Tangerine	136
6	☆	☆	DMC 745	Yellow - Light Pale	113
7	♣	♣	DMC 951	Tawny - Light	1313
8	■	■	DMC 3326	Rose - Light	36
9	♡	♡	DMC 3341	Apricot	829
10	○	○	DMC 3753	Antique Blue - Ultra Very Light	1284

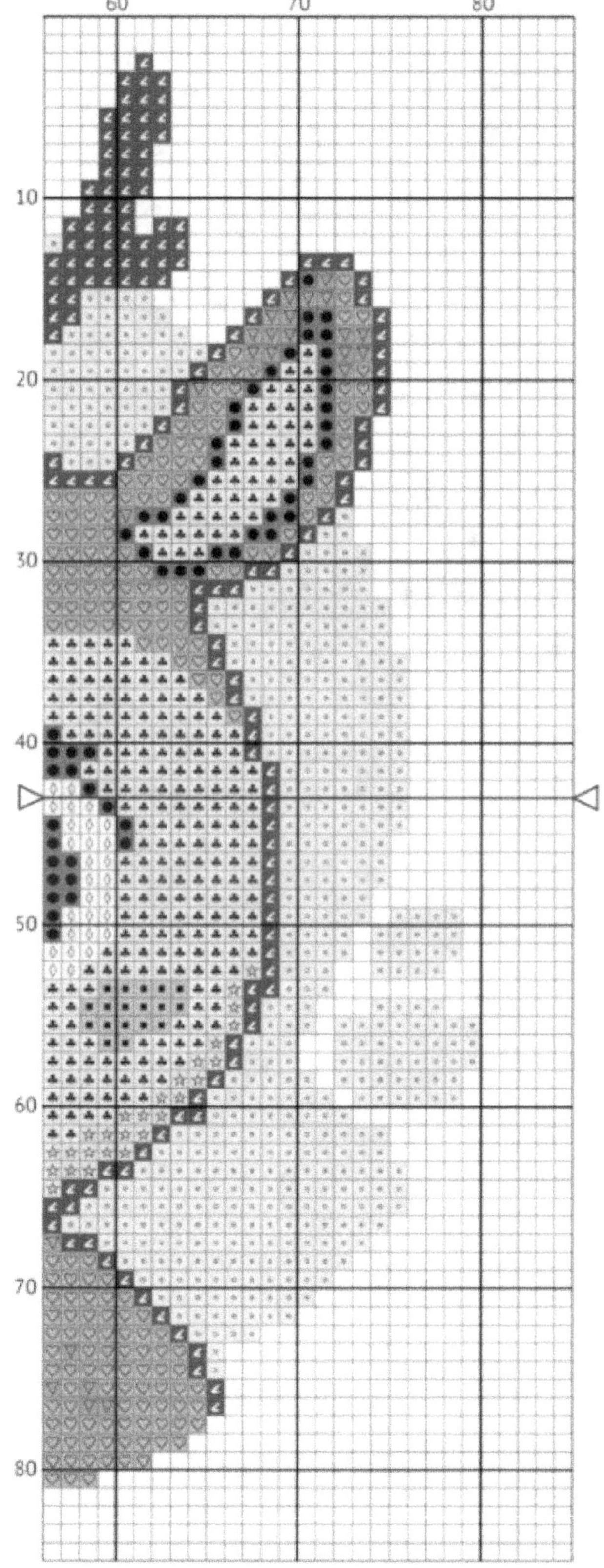

Rhino / Rinoceronte

Floss list for crosses

Use 2 strands of thread for cross stitch

N	Symbol		Number	Name	Stitches
1	≡	≡	DMC B5200	Snow White	260
2	■	■	DMC 26	Lavender - Pale	284
3	☆	☆	DMC 159	Gray Blue - Light	2
4	◣	◣	DMC 955	Nile Green - Light	1323
5	◺	◺	DMC 3747	Blue Violet - Very Light	1452
6	✾	✾	DMC 3756	Baby Blue - Ultra Very Light	23
7	♡	♥	DMC 3834	Grape - Dark	487

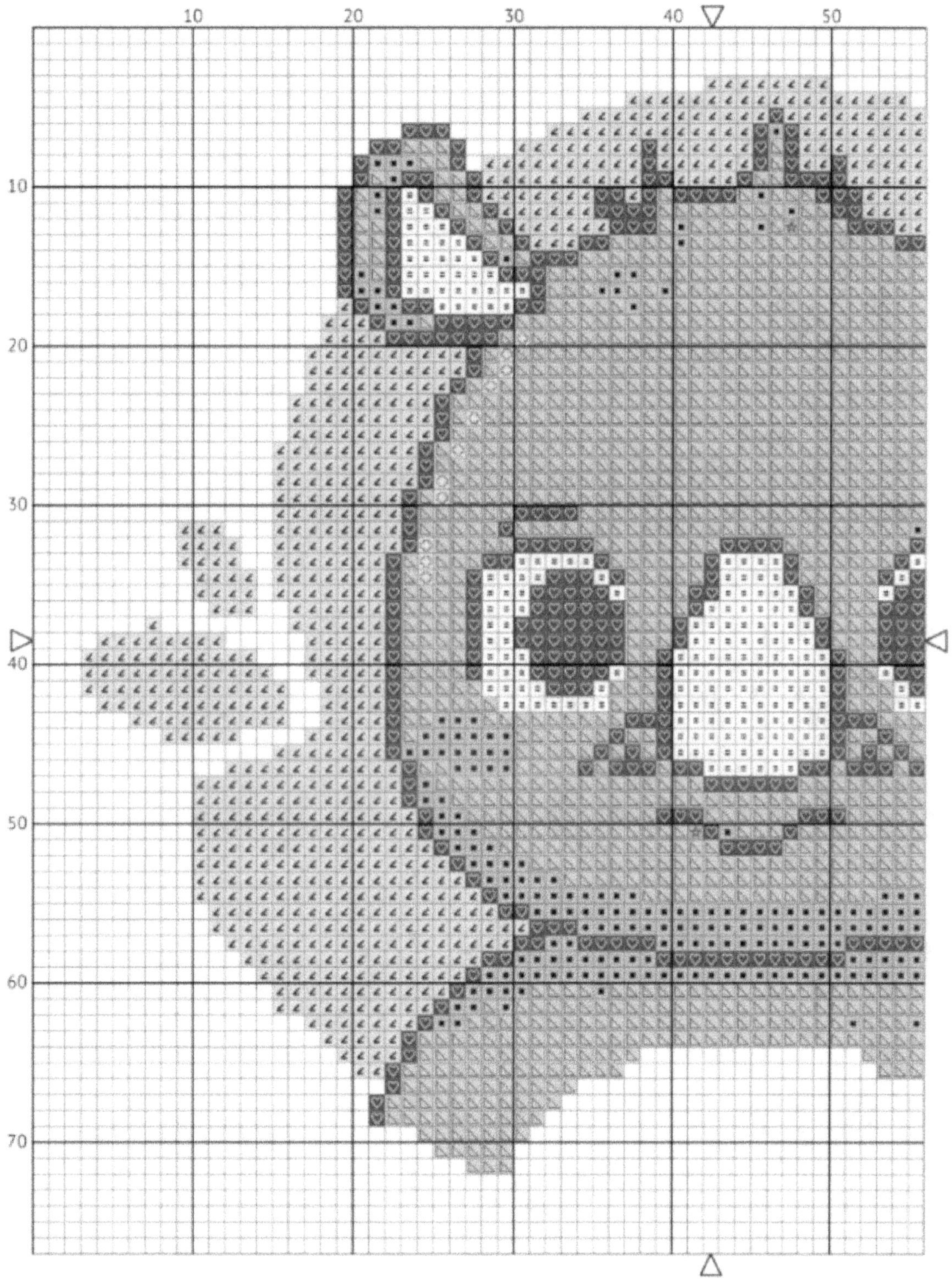

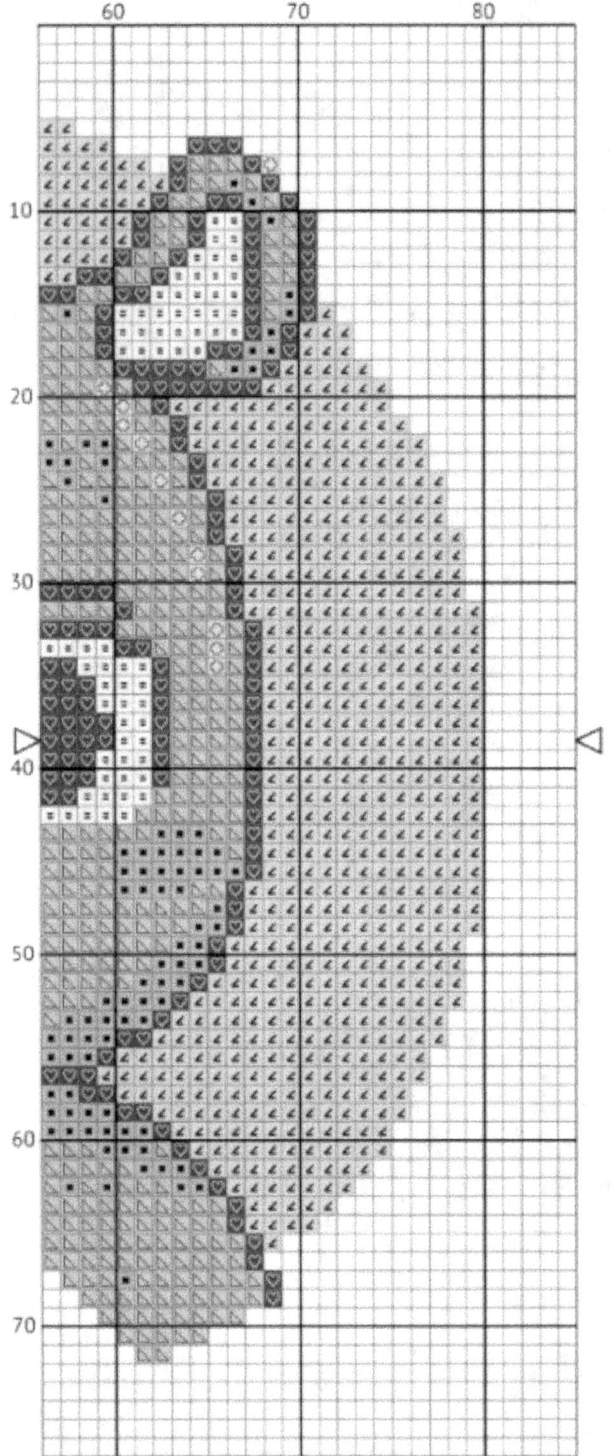

Shark / Tiburón

Design size: 85 x 81 stitches

Floss list for crosses

Use 2 strands of thread for cross stitch

N	Symbol		Number	Name	Stitches
1	✕	✕	DMC B5200	Snow White	18
2	◇	◇	DMC BLANK	White	948
3	m	m	DMC 168	Pewter - Very Light	329
4	♣	♣	DMC 963	Dusty Rose - Ultra Very Light	1358
5	◣	◣	DMC 3747	Blue Violet - Very Light	1144
6	●	◐	DMC 3834	Grape - Dark	248

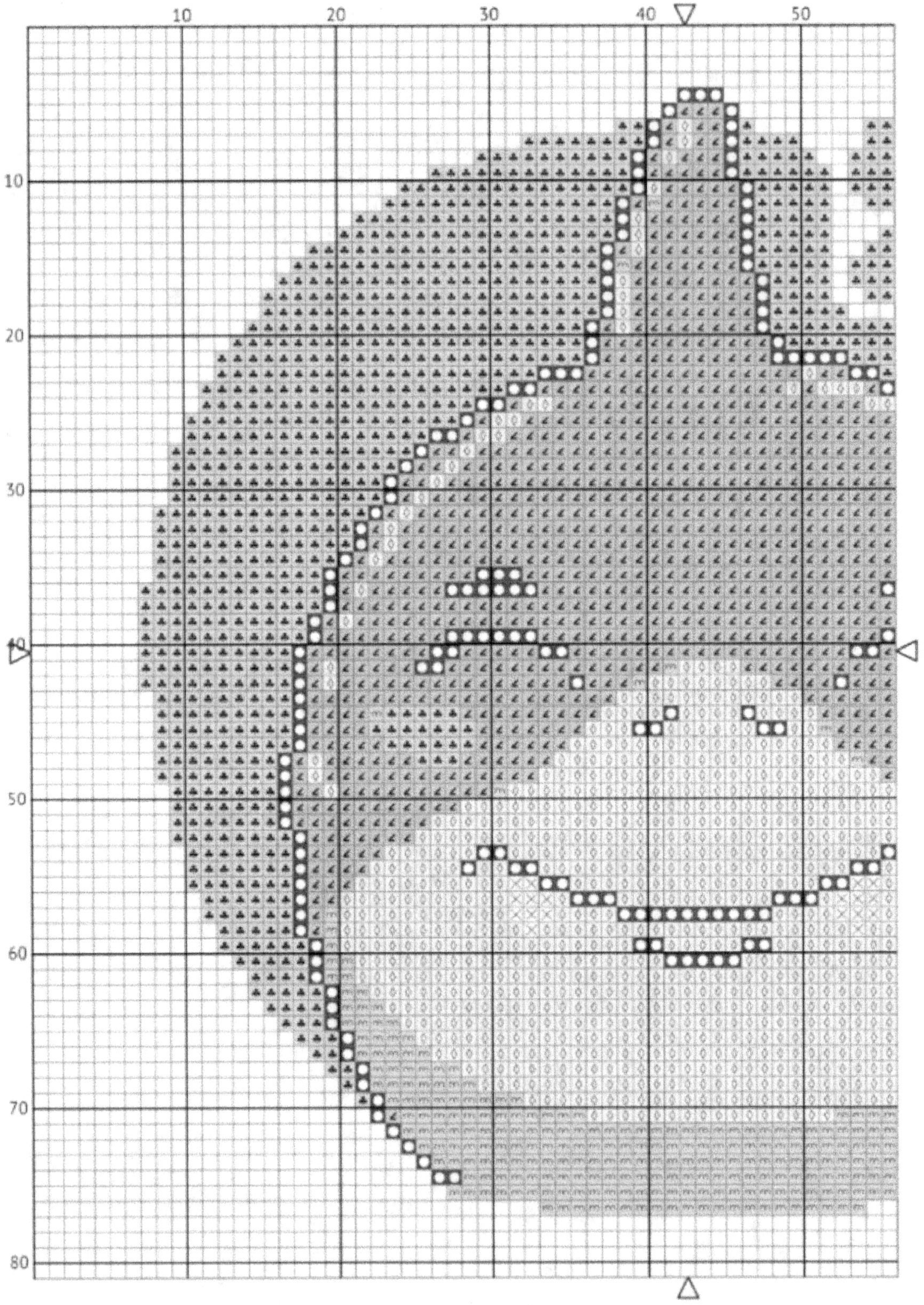

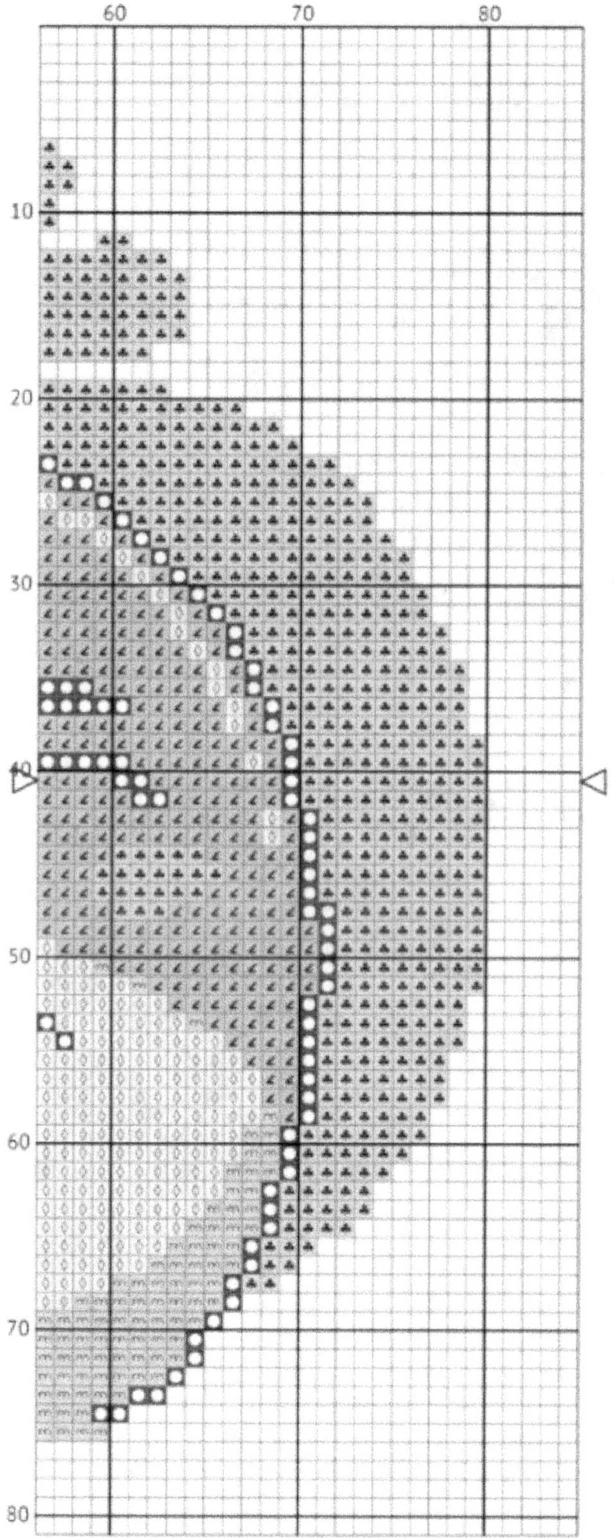

Tiger / Tigre

Design size: 85 x 81 stitches

Floss list for crosses

Use 2 strands of thread for cross stitch

N	Symbol		Number	Name	Stitches
1	☰	☰	DMC B5200	Snow White	94
2	◢	◢	DMC 210	Lavender - Medium	1636
3	●	●	DMC 746	Off White	869
4	♣	♣	DMC 777	Raspberry - Very Dark	615
5	☆	☆	DMC 956	Geranium	14
6	♡	♡	DMC 963	Dusty Rose - Ultra Very Light	42
7	m	m	DMC 972	Canary - Deep	1027
8	▽	▽	DMC 3855	Autumn Gold - Light	146

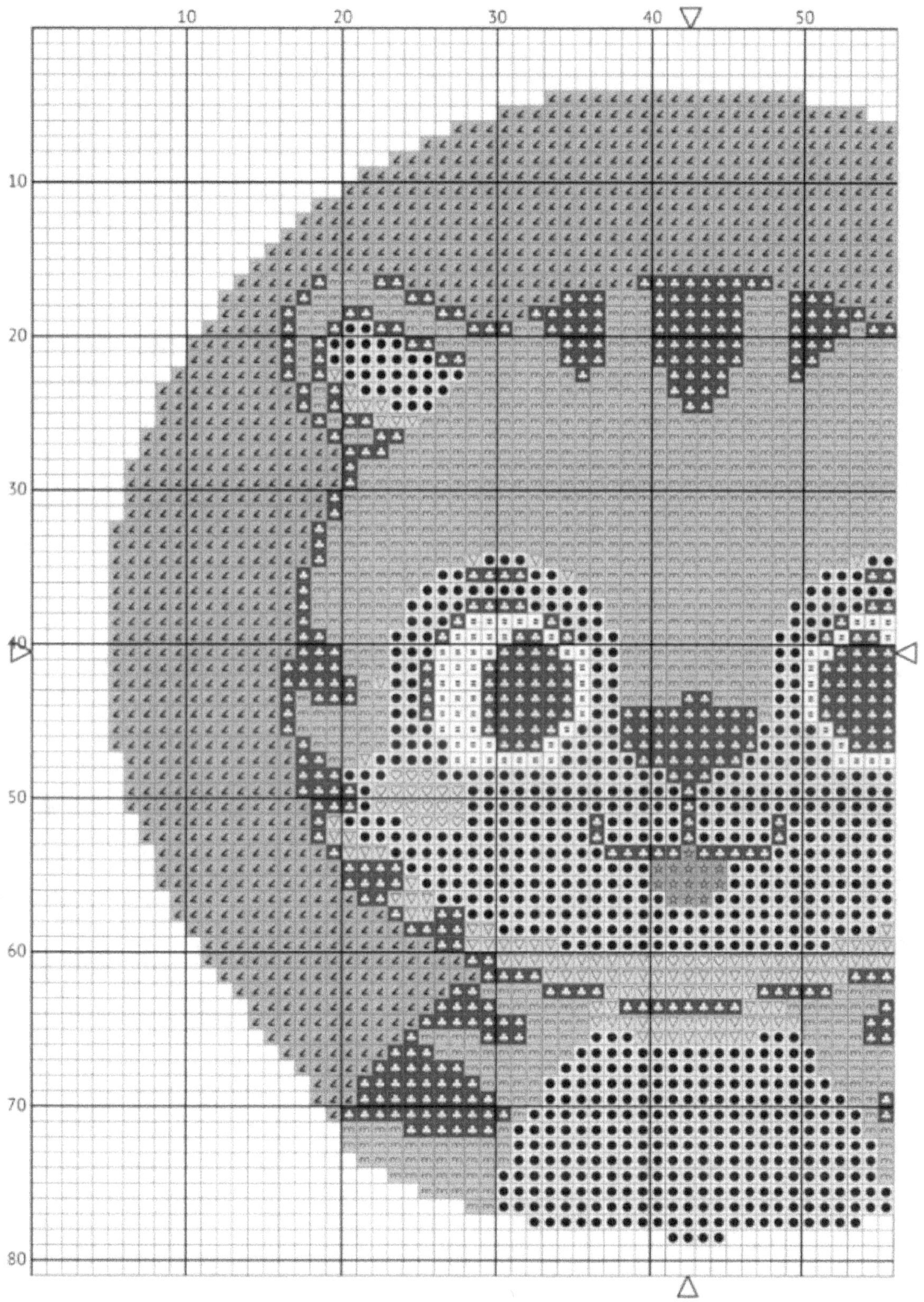

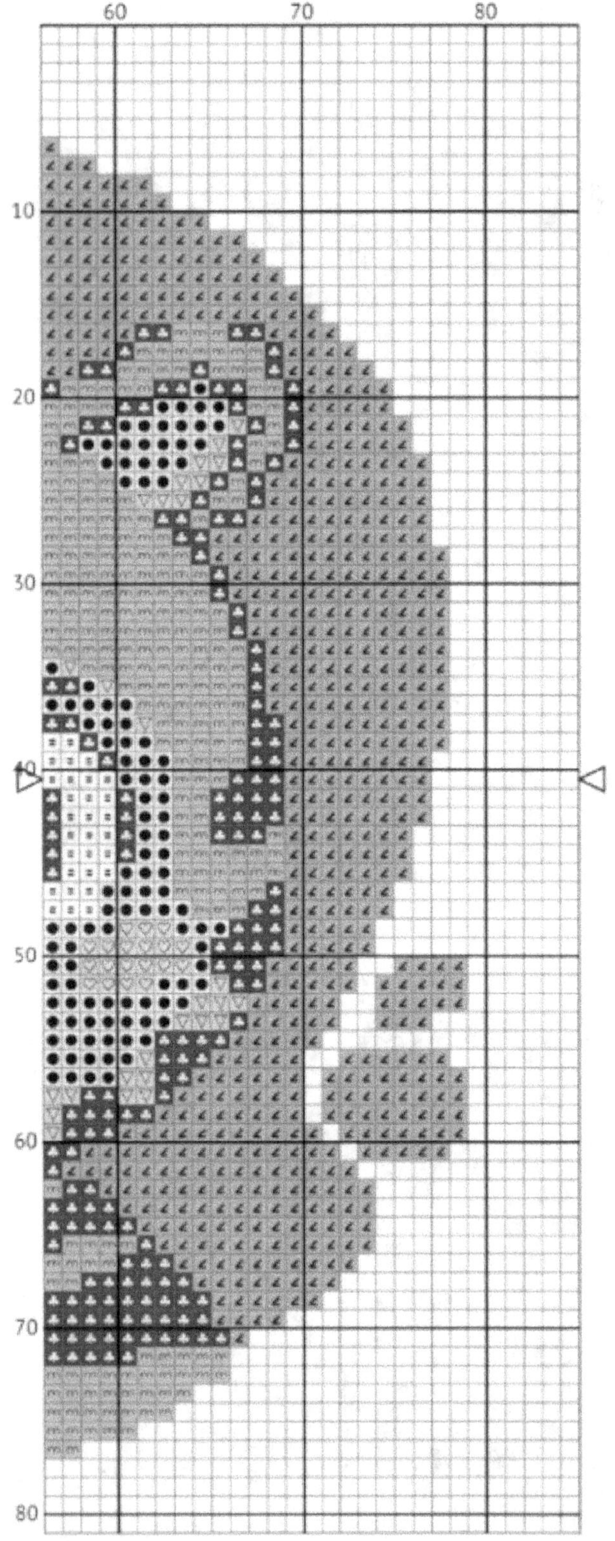

Fennec Fox / Zorro Fénec

Design size: 85 x 65 stitches

Floss list for crosses

Use 2 strands of thread for cross stitch

N	Symbol		Number	Name	Stitches
1	☆	☆	DMC B5200	Snow White	46
2	■	■	DMC 746	Off White	691
3	m	m	DMC 919	Red Copper	454
4	♣	♣	DMC 950	Desert Sand - Light	992
5	✛	✛	DMC 951	Tawny - Light	80
6	♡	♡	DMC 967	Apricot - Very Light	78
7	○	○	DMC 3689	Mauve - Light	608

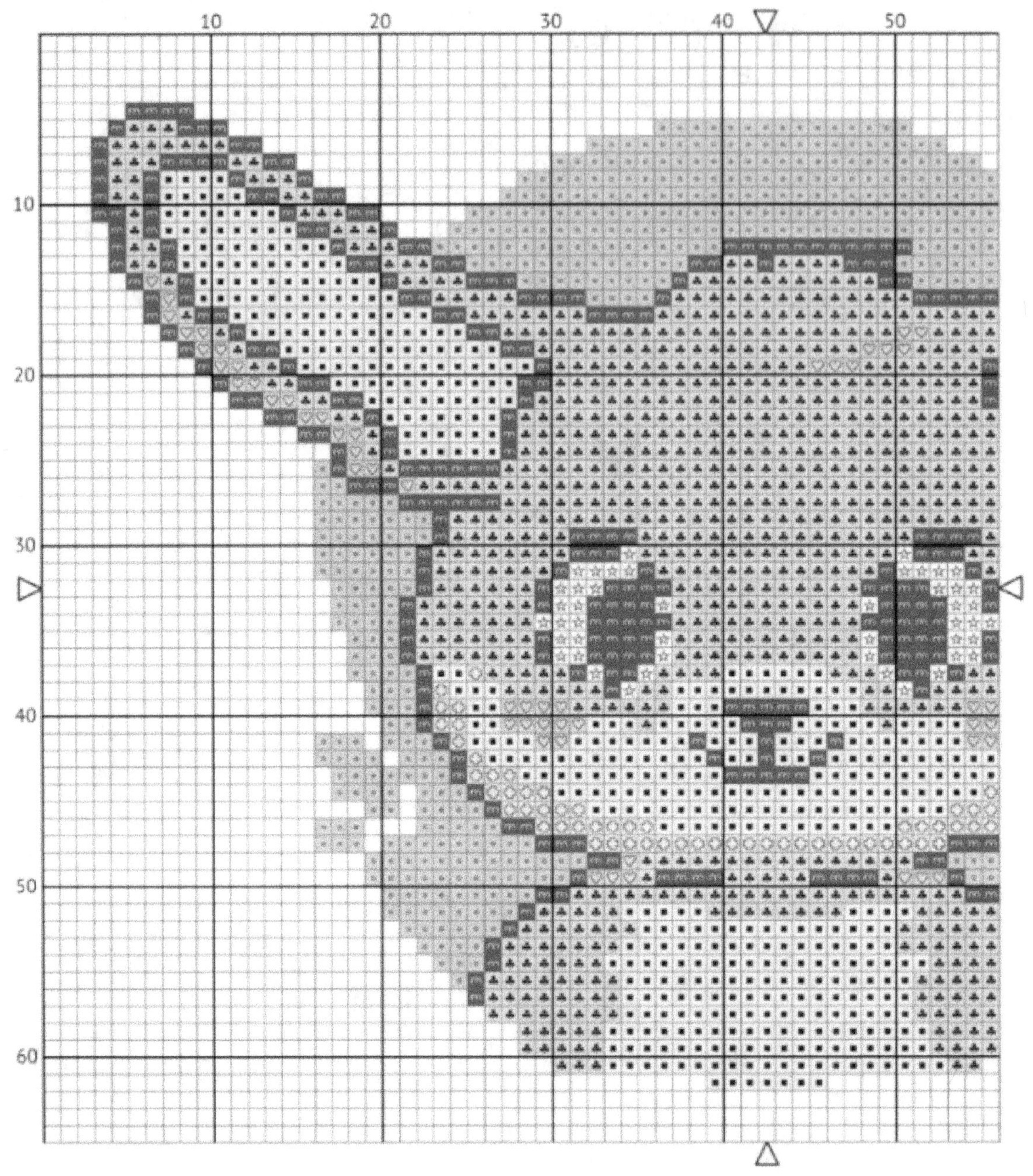

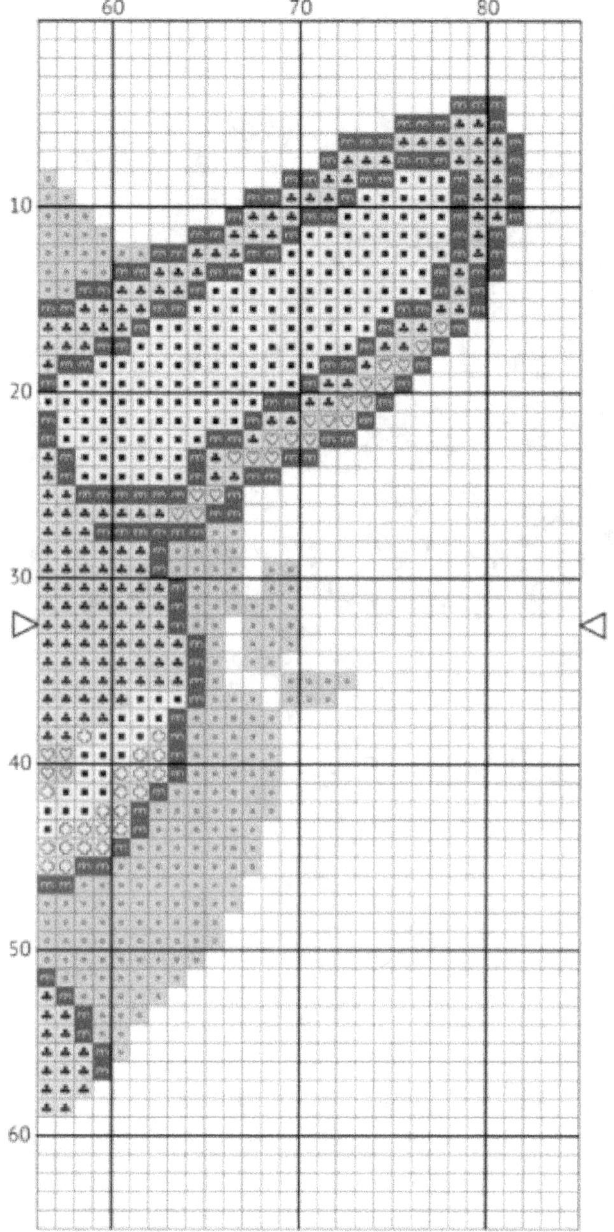

Raccoon / Mapache

Design size: 85 x 80 stitches

Floss list for crosses

Use 2 strands of thread for cross stitch

N	Symbol		Number	Name	Stitches
1	✕	✕	DMC B5200	Snow White	90
2	m	m	DMC 03	Tin - Medium	40
3	◊	◊	DMC 26	Lavender - Pale	632
4	♣	♣	DMC 30	Blueberry - Medium Light	1520
5	∠	∠	DMC 211	Lavender - Light	917
6	◺	◺	DMC 336	Navy Blue	505
7	☆	☆	DMC 3779	Rosewood - Very Light	243
8	○	○	DMC 3807	Cornflower Blue	521

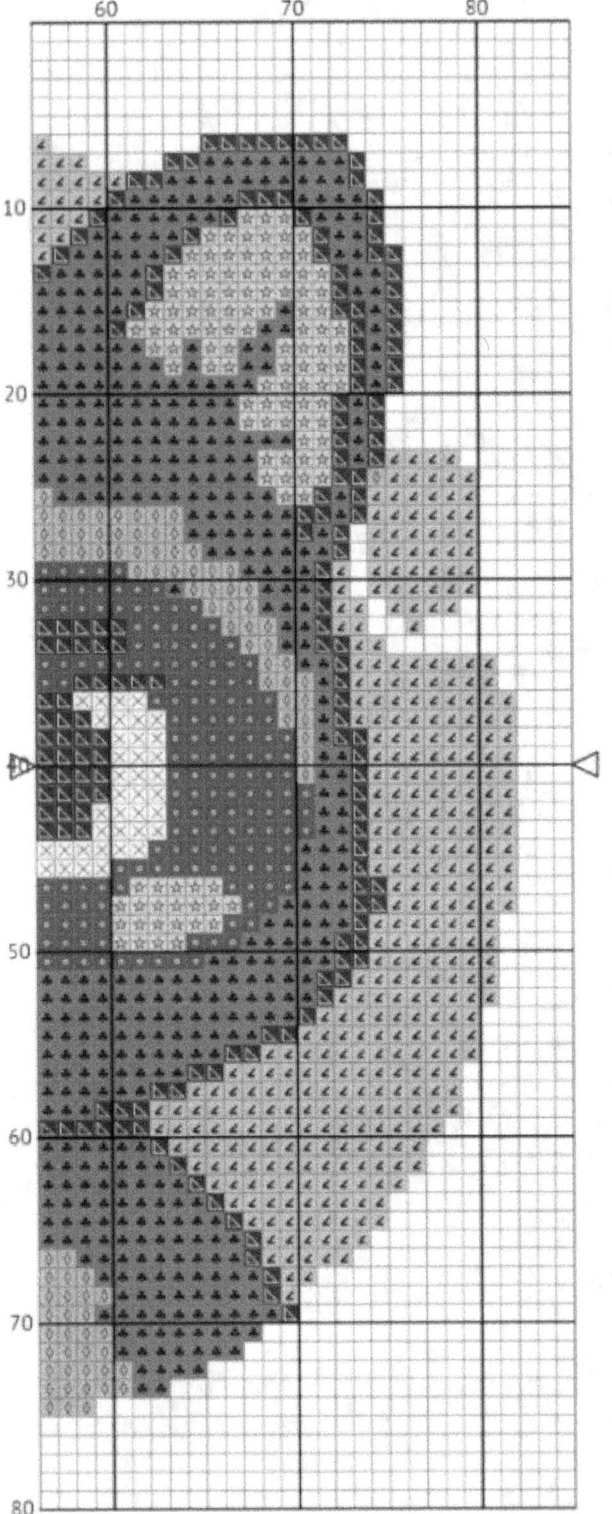

Fox / Zorro

Design size: 85 x 85 stitches

Floss list for crosses

Use 2 strands of thread for cross stitch

N	Symbol		Number	Name	Stitches
1	▽	▽	DMC B5200	Snow White	101
2	m	m	DMC 14	Apple Green - Pale	840
3	∘	∘	DMC 352	Coral - Light	1668
4	■	■	DMC 740	Tangerine	101
5	◺	◺	DMC 919	Red Copper	661
6	●	●	DMC 3779	Rosewood - Very Light	246
7	♡	♡	DMC 3823	Yellow - Ultra Pale	1039

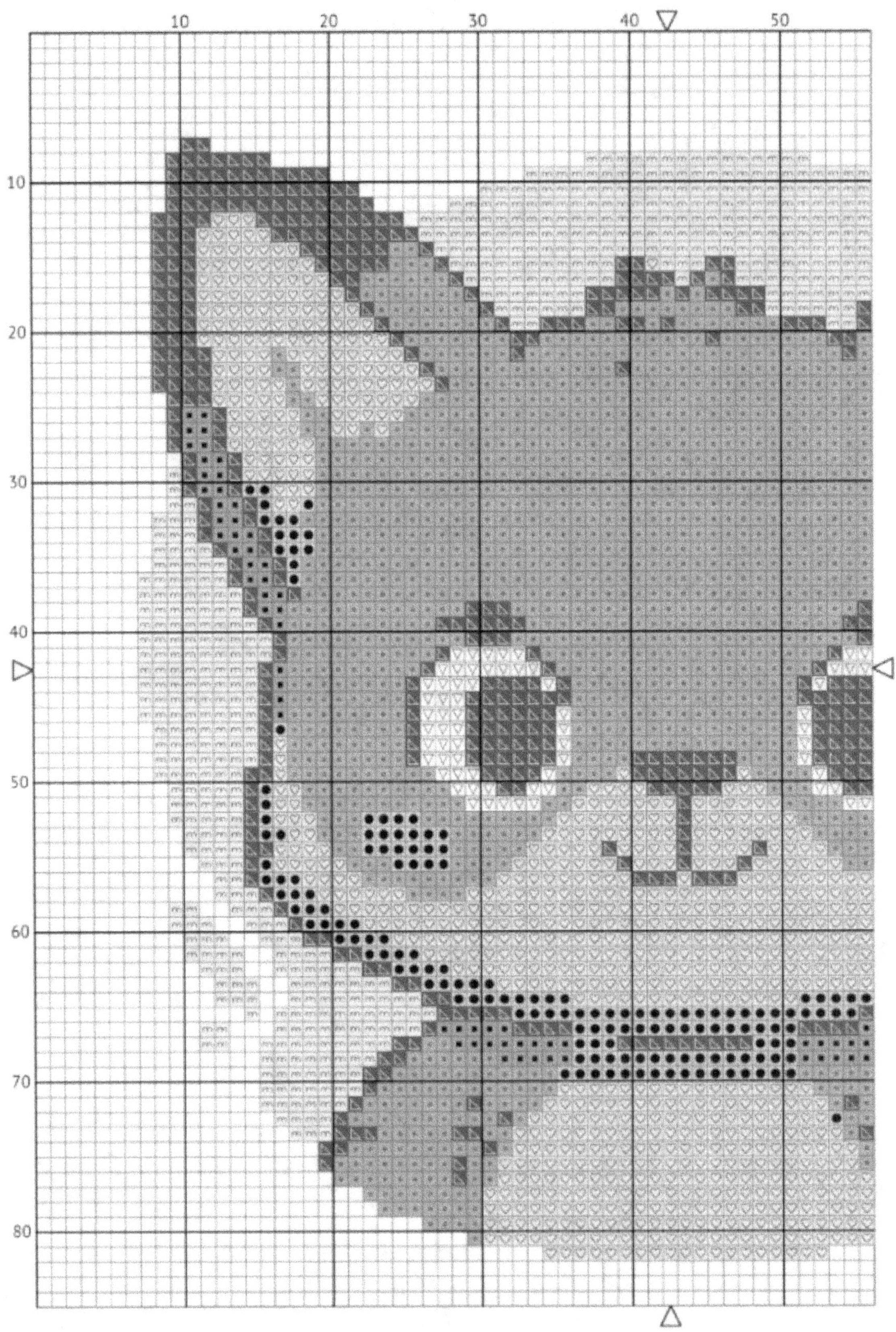

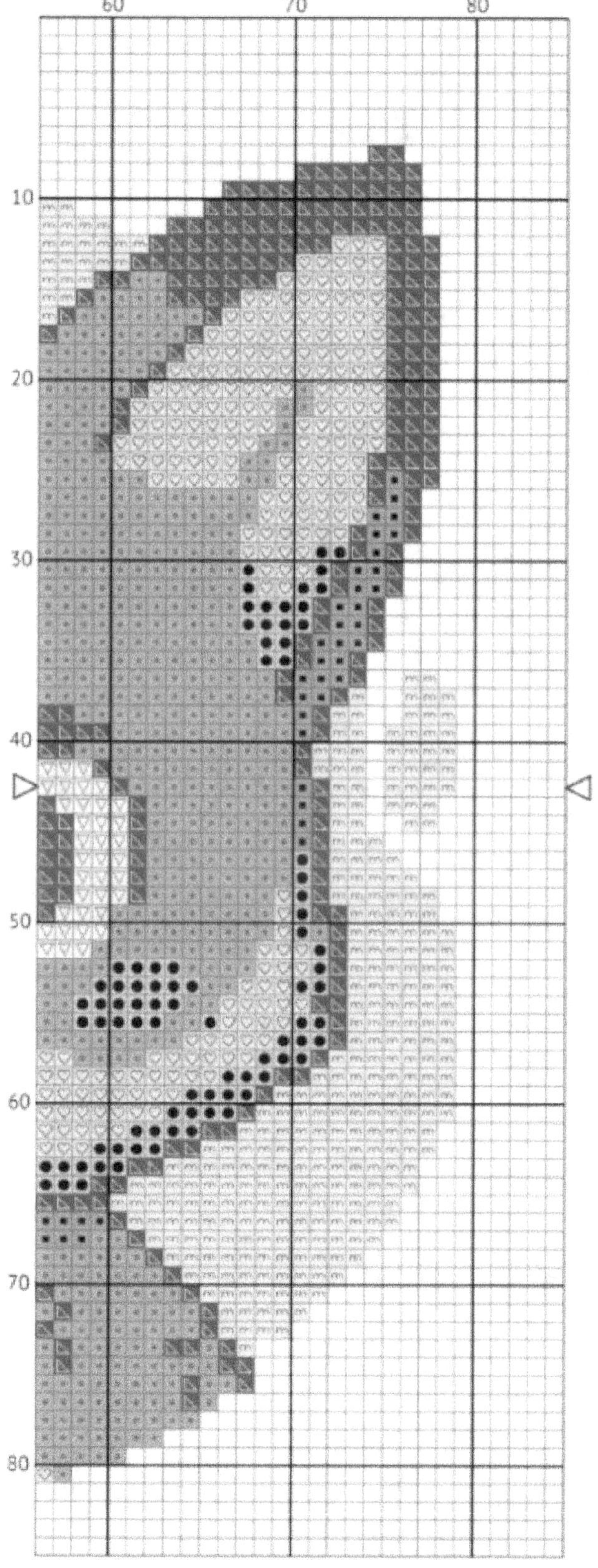